MEDIAEVAL SOURCES IN
TRANSLATION

30

BOETHIUS OF DACIA:

ON THE SUPREME GOOD, ON THE ETERNITY OF THE WORLD, ON DREAMS

Translation and Introduction

by

JOHN F. WIPPEL

PONTIFICAL INSTITUTE OF MEDIAEVAL STUDIES

CANADIAN CATALOGUING IN PUBLICATION

Boethius, of Dacia, 13th cent.
On the supreme good; On the eternity of the world; On dreams

(Mediaeval sources in translation, ISSN 0316-0874; 30)
Translation of: De summo bono; De aeternitate mundi; De somniis.
Bibliography: p.
Includes index.
ISBN 0-88844-280-7

1. Philosophy, Medieval. I. Wippel, John F. II. Pontifical Institute
of Mediaeval Studies. III. Title. IV. Title: On the eternity of the
world. V. Title: On dreams. VI. Series.

B765.B682E5 1987   180   C86-094952-4

© 1987 by

Pontifical Institute of Mediaeval Studies
59 Queen's Park Crescent East
Toronto, Ontario, Canada M5S 2C4
Printed by Les Éditions Marquis Ltée, Montmagny, Canada

Distributed outside North America by
E. J. Brill, Leiden, The Netherlands
(Brill ISBN 90 04 08321 9)

Contents

Acknowledgments

The author wishes to acknowledge that the Latin text used is that published by the Danish Society of Language and Literature in Corpus Philosophorum Danicorum Medii Aevi 6.2, *Boethii Daci Opera... Opuscula*, edited by Niels Jorgen Green-Pedersen (Copenhagen: Gad, 1976). The author also wishes to acknowledge permission from The Free Press, A Division of Macmillan, Inc., to reprint here in revised form a translation of *On the Supreme Good* which originally appeared in *Medieval Philosophy: From St. Augustine to Nicholas of Cusa*, edited by John F. Wippel and Allan B. Wolter, OFM (Copyright © 1969 by The Free Press), pp. 369-375.

Introduction

While relatively little is known about the life and career of Boethius of Dacia, considerable progress has been made in recent decades with respect to his writings. As a consequence, more light has been cast on his important role within the Faculty of Arts at the University of Paris in the early 1270s.[1] He is emerging as a leading representative of the movement often referred to as Latin Averroism or as Radical Aristotelianism which had developed there at about that time.[2] It is now clear that a number of the propositions condemned in March, 1277 by the Bishop of Paris, Stephen Tempier, were taken from his writings.[3]

---

[1] For an excellent overview of recent scholarship concerning Boethius of Dacia see J. Pinborg, "Zur Philosophie des Boethius de Dacia. Ein Uberblick," *Studia Mediewistyczne* 15 (1974), 165-185. Note the bibliography on pp. 182-185. Also see the bibliography in *Corpus Philosophorum Danicorum Medii Aevi 6.2. Boethii Daci Opera: Opuscula De aeternitate mundi, De summo bono, De somniis*, ed. N. G. Green-Pedersen (Copenhagen, 1976), pp. 468-471.

[2] For a good introduction to this general movement see F. Van Steenberghen, *La philosophie au XIIIᵉ siècle* (Louvain, 1966), CC. VIII and IX (pp. 357-493).

[3] For a brief introduction to the Condemnations of 1270 and 1277 at Paris see J. Wippel, "The Condemnations of 1270 and 1277 at Paris," *The Journal of Medieval and Renaissance Studies* 7 (1977), 169-201, along with the references given there. In addition note especially Van Steenberghen, *Maître Siger de Brabant* (Louvain-Paris, 1977), pp. 74-79, 139-176; R. Hissette, *Enquête sur les 219 articles condamnés à Paris le 7 mars 1277* (Louvain-Paris, 1977). Hissette's study focuses on the Condemnation of 1277 itself and attempts to identify, and with considerable success, the intended targets for many of the individual propositions condemned. He concludes that of these thirteen seem to be directly aimed at Boethius of Dacia, and thinks it probable that three more were also aimed at Boethius, and plausible that as many as 26 additional propositions could touch on his views (see pp. 314-315). Hissette has continued his investigations of the Condemnation of 1277 and its intended targets in subsequent publications. Note in particular his "Etienne Tempier et ses condamnations," *Recherches de Théologie ancienne et médiévale* 47 (1980), 231-270; "Albert le Grand et Thomas d'Aquin dans la censure parisienne du 7 mars 1277," in *Miscellanea Mediaevalia* 15 (1982), 226-246. See p. 233 and n. 48 on condemned propositions possibly directed at Boethius of Dacia.

Although he has been referred to as Boethius of Sweden, more recent research indicates that he hailed from Denmark.[4] The dates of his birth and death remain unknown, but it is clear that by ca. 1270 he was well enough established at Paris to serve as a Master there in the Faculty of Arts. He has been listed by some medieval manuscripts as a defender or even as a major advocate of propositions condemned in 1277, and more will be said below about this. Nonetheless, he was not cited in November, 1276, to appear before the Royal Inquisitor as were Siger of Brabant and two of his other associates from the Faculty of Arts.[5] It has been suggested that Boethius's teaching activity at Paris had already come to a halt by that date, and perhaps by 1272-1273.[6] According to an early fourteenth-century bibliographical catalogue for the Dominican Order, Boethius may have subsequently become a Dominican.[7]

If our knowledge of his career remains meager, more is now known about his writings. His very name had all but disappeared from the history of philosophy until almost 100 years ago when B. Hauréau rediscovered him, as it were, and brought his person and two of his then unedited works to the attention of the scholarly

---

[4] For the fundamental study establishing this see S. Skovgaard Jensen, ''On the National Origin of the Philosopher Boetius De Dacia,'' *Classica et Mediaevalia* 24 (1963), 232-241. Jensen's conclusion that Boethius came from Denmark rather than from Sweden has won general acceptance.

[5] On this see A. Dondaine, ''Le manuel de l'inquisiteur 1230-1330,'' *Archivum Fratrum Praedicatorum* 17 (1947), 85-194. On Siger of Brabant and this manual see pp. 186-192. For some interesting suggestions to explain why Boethius of Dacia was not cited to appear before the Inquisition insofar as one can determine from this manual see L.-J. Bataillon, ''Bulletin d'histoire des doctrines médiévales: le treizième siècle (fin),'' *Revue des Sciences Philosophiques et Théologiques* 65 (1981), 105.

[6] See Pinborg, ''Zur Philosophie des Boethius de Dacia,'' p. 165.

[7] Often referred to as the Catalogue of Stams, this *Tabula scriptorum Ordinis Praedicatorum* has twice been edited. See H. Denifle, ''Quellen zur Gelehrtengeschichte des Predigerordens im 13. und 14. Jahrhundert,'' *Archiv für Literatur- und Kirchengeschichte des Mittelalters* 2 (1886), 230, n. 35; G. Meersseman, *Laurentii Pignon Catalogi et Chronica, accedunt Catalogi Stamsensis et Upsalensis scriptorum O.P.* (Rome, 1936), pp. 64-65, n. 63. Also cf. G. Sajó, *Un traité récemment découvert de Boèce de Dacie De mundi aeternitate* (Budapest, 1954), pp. 18-19.

world.[8] In 1924 M. Grabmann discovered two other interesting small treatises by Boethius, his *De summo bono* and his *De somniis*, and subsequently edited them.[9] Important though these two writings are for our understanding of Boethius's philosophical thought, their contents were hardly sufficient to account for the fact that Boethius had been named as one of the major defenders of the propositions condemned in 1277.[10]

The reasons for this have become somewhat clearer with the publication by G. Sajó of another work mentioned in a listing of his writings in the Catalogue of Stams, that is, his *De aeternitate mundi*. This gave renewed impetus to scholarly interest in Boethius of Dacia and his role in the controversies at Paris in the early 1270s. While no one has seriously challenged the authenticity of this work, the interpretation of it proposed by Sajó regarding Boethius's solution to the faith-reason problem provoked considerable negative reaction.

---

[8] See B. Hauréau, ''Un des hérétiques condamnés à Paris en 1277,'' *Journal des Savants* (1886), 176-183; ''Boetius, maître ès arts à Paris,'' *Histoire littéraire de la France* 30 (1888), 270-279. The works discovered in manuscript by Hauréau were Boethius's *Commentary on the Topics* and his *De modis significandi*.

[9] See M. Grabmann, *Neuaufgefundene Werke des Siger von Brabant und Boetius von Dacien*, Sitzungsberichte der Bayerischen Akademie der Wissenschaften. Philosophisch-historische Abteilung, 1924, 2 (Munich, 1924). For his edition of these two works see ''Die opuscula *De summo bono sive de vita philosophi* und *De sompniis* des Boetius von Dacien,'' *Archives d'Histoire Doctrinale et Littéraire du Moyen Âge* 6 (1932), 287-317; *Mittelalterliches Geistesleben* 2 (Munich, 1936), pp. 200-224.

[10] As will be noted below, it does seem that a few of the propositions condemned in 1277 were aimed at one or the other of these two treatises. For medieval manuscript references to Boethius as a major defender of the propositions condemned in 1277 see the citations in Sajó, *Un traité récemment découvert*, p. 17. Thus at the end of one of the oldest listings of the condemned articles we read that the ''main defender of these articles was a certain cleric named Boetus'' (Paris, Bibliothèque Nationale, lat. 16533, f. 60). Another Paris manuscript (Bibliothèque Nationale, lat. 4391, f. 68) lists the prohibited propositions under the rubric: ''Against the heretics Siger and Boethius.'' And in another Paris manuscript containing a catalogue of the works of Raymond Lull, his polemical *Declaratio per modum dialogi edita contra aliquorum philosophorum et eorum sequacium opiniones erroneas et damnatas a venerabili Patre Domino Episcopo Parisiensi* is referred to as his ''Book against the errors of Boethius and Siger'' (Bibliothèque Nationale, lat. 15.450, f. 80). These citations are also given in *Boethii Daci Opera Modi Significandi sive Quaestiones super Priscianum Maiorem*, ed. by J. Pinborg and H. Roos with S. Skovgaard Jensen, Corpus Philosophorum Danicorum Medii Aevi 4.1 (Copenhagen, 1969), p. xxxi.

Sajó had mistakenly concluded that Boethius defended the infamous "double-truth" theory in this work, though Sajó eventually reversed his interpretation.[11] In 1964 Sajó produced a much improved edition of the same text on the strength of other and more reliable manuscripts which had by then come to light.[12] And still more recently, all of the works mentioned so far, along with several others, have been edited in the series *Corpus Philosophorum Danicorum Medii Aevi*.[13]

If one may judge both from the works of Boethius which have survived in manuscript and which have now been edited, and from the titles of other works assigned to him by the Stams Catalogue or else mentioned by Boethius himself in his extant writings,[14] his literary activity ranged widely over most of the general areas of philosophy. His writings include a series of Commentaries on Aristotle

---

[11] For this see Sajó, *Un traité récemment découvert*, pp. 36-37, 71-79. He was originally followed in seeing in this treatise a defense of the "double-truth theory" by F. Sassen, "Boethius van Dacie en de Theorie van de dubbele waarheid," *Studia Catholica* 30 (1955), 266-273. This interpretation was quickly challenged, among others by E. Gilson, "Boèce de Dacie et la double vérité," *Archives d'Histoire Doctrinale et Littéraire du Moyen Âge* 20 (1955), 81-99; A. Maurer, "Boethius of Dacia and the Double Truth," *Mediaeval Studies* 17 (1955), 235-239; F. Van Steenberghen, "Nouvelles recherches sur Siger de Brabant et son école," *Revue philosophique de Louvain* 54 (1956), 137-147; *La philosophie au XIIIe siècle*, pp. 404-412; "Une légende tenace: la théorie de la double vérité," in *Académie royale de Belgique, Bulletin de la Classe des Lettres et des Sciences morales et politiques*, sér. V, 56 (1970), 184-88; *Thomas Aquinas and Radical Aristotelianism* (Washington, D.C., 1980), pp. 95-99; P. Wilpert, "Boethius von Dacien — die Autonomie des Philosophen," *Miscellanea Mediaevalia* 3 (Berlin, 1964), 135-152; H. Schrödter, "Boetius von Dacien und die Autonomie des Wissens. Ein Fund und seine Bedeutung," *Theologie und Philosophie* 47 (1972), 16-35. For Sajó's rejection of his original interpretation see his "Boetius de Dacia und seine philosophische Bedeutung," *Miscellanea Mediaevalia* 2 (Berlin, 1963), 454-463, esp. 458-460.

[12] *Boetii de Dacia Tractatus De Aeternitate Mundi* (Berlin, 1964).

[13] See note 1 above for this edition of Boethius's *De aeternitate mundi, De summo bono, and De somniis,* and note 10 for the edition of his *De modis significandi (Modi significandi)* including both the full version and an important *abbreviatio* of it by Godfrey of Fontaines. See Vol. 6.1 in the same series for his Questions on the *Topics: Quaestiones super librum Topicorum*, ed. by N. G. Green-Pedersen and J. Pinborg (Copenhagen, 1976).

[14] For a listing taken from all of these sources see Pinborg, "Zur Philosophie des Boethius de Dacia," pp. 166-168. Also see Sajó, "Boetius de Dacia und seine philosophische Bedeutung," pp. 454ff., 460-462.

(written in the form of questions), various works treating of logic and of speculative grammar, some questions on ethical topics, a *Metaphysics*, and other writings devoted to particular subjects such as the three treatises translated here and mentioned above. Rather than attempt to offer any overall summary of his thought, these introductory remarks will be limited to the contents of these three treatises: *On the Supreme Good (De summo bono), On the Eternity of the World (De aeternitate mundi),* and *On Dreams (De somniis).* Examination of these works is sufficient to reveal that Boethius was a philosopher of considerable stature, and one who could write with great precision. This impression is only confirmed by consultation of his other published works. Moreover, a brief survey of the contents of these three treatises will suffice to show why Boethius is linked by certain medieval manuscripts with the Condemnation of 1277. Whether or not each of the particular propositions which seems to be taken from his writings deserves such condemnation when it is read in its original context is, of course, another matter.

On The Supreme Good[15]

This small treatise starts out innocently enough, but has been subject to widely divergent interpretations. Boethius states that his purpose here is to determine by reason what is the supreme good available for human beings. He quickly argues that this good must belong to man by means of his highest power, that is, his intellect. Boethius distinguishes between man's intellective power insofar as it is speculative and insofar as it is practical. The supreme good available to man in terms of his speculative intellect is knowledge of truth and delight in the same. This includes knowledge of all beings which are caused by the First Being, knowledge of the First Being itself, and delight in all of this. The supreme good accessible to man in

---

[15] Other titles are less frequently assigned to this work within the manuscript tradition, including ''The Proper Life for Philosophers,'' ''On the Human Good,'' and ''The Life of the Philosopher.'' See *Corpus Philosophorum Danicorum Medii Aevi 6.2,* p. xlvii. As G. Wieland has pointed out, these titles also accurately reflect the contents of the treatise. See his *Ethica — Scientia Practica. Die Anfänge der philosophischen Ethik im 13. Jahrhundert,* Beiträge zur Geschichte der Philosophie und Theologie des Mittelalters, Neue Folge, 21 (Münster Westfalen, 1981), p. 213.

terms of his practical intellect is right action, that is, doing what is good and taking delight in it.

By combining these two, the theoretical and the practical, Boethius concludes that the supreme good available for man is to know the true, to do the good, and to take delight in both. This, he continues, is the very essence of the good life or, as he puts it, the happy life. And, he adds, one who shares more fully in such happiness draws closer to "that happiness which we expect in the life to come on the authority of faith."[16] This passage should be noted since it is the only explicit reference in this treatise either to faith or to life after death.

Since so great a good is available for man, continues Boethius, all of man's distinctively human actions should be directed to it, that is, to knowledge of the true and doing the good. All of the happy man's actions should be in accord with his pursuit of this supreme good. Actions which are opposed to this or even acts which are indifferent to man's attainment of it are sinful. All such sinful actions result from inordinate desire. This, comments Boethius somewhat sadly, is why only the smallest number of men really succeed in pursuing wisdom. The vast majority are barred from this by their inordinate desires. This accounts for their pursuit of a life of laziness, or of sense pleasure, or of riches.

The small number of men who do successfully pursue the true supreme good should be held in high honor, continues Boethius. They should be honored because they pursue the pleasure of reason and despise pleasures of the senses and, therefore, because they alone live according to the natural order. It is according to that order for the lower to be ordered to the higher, the nutritive to the sensitive, the sensitive to the intellective, and within the intellective realm, the practical to the theoretical. Such men, argues Boethius, are the philosophers, for they live according to the natural order.

From the moral standpoint, comments Boethius, the philosopher is virtuous, first of all because he correctly recognizes what is virtuous and noble, and what is base. Hence the philosopher can more easily choose the former and reject the latter. As Boethius puts it: "He does not sin against the natural order." Again, because the philosopher

---

[16] See below, p. 29.

has tasted the greatest pleasure — theoretical consideration of the truths of beings, he is in position to look down upon lesser pleasures such as those of sense.

Given all of this, Boethius reasons that man's desire for truth will never be fully satisfied until he arrives at knowledge of God, the uncaused cause. One reaches such knowledge by studying the caused beings of this world and their relationships to one another, and by ascending upwards to their causes, until one eventually arrives at knowledge of the First Cause. Because speculative knowledge gives great pleasure, the philosopher leads the life of greatest pleasure, especially to the degree that he attains to knowledge of this supreme being. Boethius also maintains that the philosopher can discover that all other being in the universe depends upon the First Cause. In other words, Boethius is not content to reduce the First Principle which is discovered by the philosopher to the level of a mere First Mover.

Having discovered all of these things about the First Cause, the philosopher is moved to wonder at it and to love it. All of this, insists Boethius, is in accord with nature and with right reason. This, then, is the life of greatest pleasure, because it leads one to the object of supreme pleasure, that is, the First Principle, and to delight in it and in its goodness. In fact, anyone who does not lead such a life does not live rightly. Boethius softens this last remark by observing that by a philosopher he has in mind anyone who lives in accord with nature and who has attained this best and ultimate end of human living — God.

As E. Gilson remarked some thirty years ago, this treatise has been interpreted in diametrically opposed ways.[17] Some have seen in it a defense of the purest kind of rationalism.[18] Others find nothing in it which is contrary to Christian faith. Rather it simply presents itself as a purely philosophical discussion of the supreme good for

---

[17] *History of Christian Philosophy in the Middle Ages* (New York, 1955), p. 401.

[18] See in particular P. Mandonnet, ''Note complémentaire sur Boèce de Dacie,'' *Revue des Sciences Philosophiques et Théologiques* 22 (1933), 250. For another more recent nuanced but critical appraisal of the contents of this treatise see R.-A. Gauthier, ''Notes sur Siger de Brabant: II. Siger en 1272-1275, Aubry de Reims et la scission des Normands,'' *Revue des Sciences Philosophiques et Théologiques* 68 (1984), 20.

man. [19] If there is almost no reference in it to man's supernatural end, this is understandable because of the treatise's avowedly philosophical nature: "By reason let us seek to determine what the supreme good is which is accessible to man." Moreover, as already mentioned above, there is one reference to religious belief in a greater happiness in the life to come.

Still, the work does seem to exhibit a certain kind of what might be called philosophical imperialism. Because of this, some contemporary interpreters find its rationalism and naturalism too extreme for one who also professes to be a believing Christian. [20] The treatise does not acknowledge, they can point out, that for the religious believer there is a higher kind of life available for man even here and now, whether this be that of the saint, or the mystic, or the theologian. Boethius's solitary reference to a greater happiness in the life to come which the Christian awaits on the testimony of faith hardly allows for this.

And thus some doubt may remain for today's reader. Does Boethius adopt such exclusive claims for philosophy in this treatise merely because he is writing as a pure philosopher? Or does the position which he develops here also reflect his personal attitude? If so, the life of the philosopher would be the highest possible kind of life for everyone, including the Christian. Little or no place would be left for the theologian or the religious saint or the mystic to claim that his is an even higher kind of life or, for that matter, that it is even defensible as a good life for man. Only the philosopher lives as man should live! In Boethius's defense, however, we should recall a principle we shall find him stressing in the next two treatises to be

---

[19] See, for instance, Van Steenberghen, *La philosophie au XIIIe siècle*, p. 404; R. Hissette, *Enquête sur les 219 articles condamnés à Paris*, pp. 17-18. Hissette does acknowledge that Boethius's way of expressing his position was bound to be offensive to theologians. If this treatise was written after 1 April 1272, Boethius would have had an additional reason for not addressing himself to questions relating to man's supernatural destiny. On that date a majority of the Arts Faculty at Paris promulgated a regulation which prohibited Masters or Bachelors of Arts from determining and even from disputing questions of a purely theological nature. See Hissette, p. 17, n. 15. Cf. Wippel, "The Condemnations of 1270 and 1277," p. 184. For the decree see H. Denifle and A. Chatelain, *Chartularium Universitatis Parisiensis* (Paris, 1889), 1: 499-500, n. 441.

[20] See the references given in n. 18 above.

examined: one who practices a given discipline, in this case philosophy itself, can do so only in light of and in accord with the principles of that discipline. When Boethius writes as a philosopher, for him to draw upon anything which he accepts solely on the strength of his religious belief would be to violate that principle.

This not withstanding, a negative implication was drawn from Boethius's treatise by some of his contemporaries. Thus one of the propositions condemned by Stephen Tempier in 1277 seems to be taken from this treatise. It reads: "There is no more excellent kind of life than to give oneself to philosophy."[21] The reader may determine for himself whether or not this condemned article accurately reflects Boethius's personal position.

Various writers have also seen some reference to this same treatise in a second article condemned by Tempier. "Only the philosophers are the wise men of this world."[22] While this article does capture something of the spirit of Boethius's *On the Supreme Good*, its language seems to reflect more directly a remark in his treatise *On the Eternity of the World*.[23] Hence we now turn to that treatise.

ON THE ETERNITY OF THE WORLD

Reference has already been made to the modern recovery of this work and the discussion which followed upon its first edition in 1954.[24] While it is generally acknowledged today that this treatise does not defend a double-truth theory, it does contain a subtle and highly original solution to the faith-reason problem. Boethius works

---

[21] See article 40 according to the numbering found in H. Denifle and A. Chatelain, *Chartularium Universitatis Parisiensis* (Paris, 1889), 1: 543-561. For another listing reorganized in systematic fashion see P. Mandonnet, *Siger de Brabant et l'averroïsme latin au XIIIᵉ siècle*, 2d ed., 2 vols. (Louvain, 1911, 1908), 2: 175-191. According to Mandonnet's numbering this is proposition 1. For an English translation which follows the Mandonnet ordering see E. Fortin and P. O'Neill in *Medieval Political Philosophy: A Sourcebook*, ed. by R. Lerner and M. Mahdi (New York, 1963), pp. 337-354. For another English translation which follows the same order see J. Wellmuth, in *Philosophy in the West: Readings in Ancient and Medieval Philosophy*, ed. by J. Katz and R. Weingartner (New York, 1966), pp. 532-542.

[22] See article 154 (*Chartularium*)/article 2 (Mandonnet).

[23] For the connection between this article and Boethius's *De aeternitate mundi* see Hissette, *Enquête*, p. 19; Gauthier, "Notes sur Siger de Brabant," p. 19, n. 30.

[24] See above, pp. 3-4 and notes 11 and 12.

out this solution in the course of attempting to show that Christian belief that the world began to be is not incompatible with what philosophers have held about the eternity of the world. In doing this he also advances some personal views about the degree of certitude which attaches to the conclusions and even to the first principles of the particular branches of theoretical philosophy, especially natural philosophy.

Boethius begins by explicitly recognizing the distinction between faith and reason. Certain things can be accepted only on the strength of the Law (revelation). No attempt should be made to demonstrate such positions on philosophical grounds. Other things which are not self-evident in themselves do admit of rational argumentation in their support. Given this, Boethius indicates that here he intends to bring into harmony the view of Christian faith concerning the eternity of the world and the position held by Aristotle and other philosophers. He offers three reasons for making this effort: 1. in order to protect the position advanced by faith; 2. in order to defend the position of the philosophers to the extent that conclusive rational argumentation can be offered in support of this; 3. in order to show that faith and philosophy do not contradict one another with respect to the issue of eternity of the world and, he adds, to undercut the arguments of certain heretics who defend the world's eternity.

Boethius then proceeds in good scholastic fashion to line up a series of arguments for each side. First he presents arguments which may be offered to prove that the world is not eternal, that is, that it began to be. Following upon this, arguments are offered for the contrary position, and this in two steps. First of all, arguments are presented to show that an eternal world is possible. These are followed by another series of arguments which attempt to show that the world in fact is eternal. While many of these arguments are highly interesting in themselves, individual examination of them will be left to the reader.

In developing his own solution to the general issue of eternity or noneternity of the world, Boethius strongly affirms the philosopher's right to discuss any question which can be disputed by rational argumentation.[25] If philosophy studies about being, the various parts of philosophy consider the various parts or kinds of being. But every question which can be disputed by rational argumentation falls within some part of being. Since the philosopher investigates all being, natural, mathematical, and divine, it belongs to him to determine every question which can be disputed by rational argumentation. Here Boethius has in mind the classical division of theoretical philosophy into its three parts, physics, mathematics, and divine science.[26]

Boethius next proceeds to show that of the three parts of theoretical philosophy, none can prove that the world began to be. That the natural philosopher cannot do this follows from two premises. First of all, one who is a specialist in a given science can demonstrate, concede, or deny something only in terms of the principles of that science. Secondly, if nature is not the first principle in the unqualified sense, it is the first principle for natural things and, therefore, the first principle which the natural philosopher can examine. Hence, so

[25] For this see below, p. 46. Boethius make this same point again somewhat farther on in this same treatise (see below, p. 55): "There is no question whose conclusion can be established by reason which the philosopher should not dispute and determine insofar as such is possible to reason." Condemned proposition 145 (Mandonnet, article 6) from Stephen Tempier's list in 1277 seems to be directed against this claim by Boethius and very likely against its formulation in this treatise. For discussion and for texts from other works where Boethius defends the same view see Hissette, *Enquête sur les 219 articles*, pp. 23-26. As Hissette points out, and rightly in my opinion, as Boethius himself defends this position it merely asserts the universal competence of the philosopher in matters which can be determined by rational argumentation. So understood, it does not eliminate the possibility of religious faith or a science based on faith, that is, theology. Hence, when read in context, it does not merit condemnation from the standpoint of Christian orthodoxy. As formulated in Tempier's list the article reads: "That there is no question which can be disputed by reason which the philosopher should not dispute and determine, because rational arguments (*rationes*) are taken from things. But it belongs to philosophy according to its various parts to consider all things."

[26] A seminal if difficult text advancing this threefold division of theoretical philosophy is Aristotle's *Metaphysics* 6, 1. Another important text for transmitting this to the Latin West is Boethius's *De Trinitate*, c. 2. See *Boethius. The Theological Tractates. The Consolation of Philosophy*, by H. F. Stewart, E. K. Rand, and S. J. Tester (Cambridge, Mass., 1978), p. 8. For an extended development of all of this see Thomas Aquinas, *Expositio super librum Boethii De Trinitate*, ed. B. Decker (Leiden, 1959), QQ. 5 and 6, and the English translation by A. Maurer, *St. Thomas Aquinas: The Division and Methods of the Sciences*, 3d rev. ed. (Toronto, 1963).

far as the natural philosopher is concerned, he must hold that nature cannot cause any new motion unless another motion which serves as its cause precedes it. But no other motion can be prior to the first motion, since otherwise it would not be first. Therefore, according to his principles, the first of which is nature, the natural philosopher cannot hold that the first motion began to be. In other words, if the first motion in the order of causal dependency is truly first, it cannot itself have begun to be. Otherwise some prior motion would have preceded it. Hence the natural philosopher, by reasoning according to the principles of his own science, cannot hold that the first motion ever began to be. This is why Aristotle concludes in Book VIII of the *Physics* that the first motion is eternal. From all of this Boethius concludes that the natural philosopher *qua* natural philosopher cannot establish the existence of any first mobile thing which began to be. Therefore he cannot show that the world began to be.

From this Boethius concludes that the natural philosopher is unable even to take up the issue of creation. Nature produces its every effect from a subject and from matter. Such production is not creation but generation. And since the production of the world in terms of its very being is not generation but creation, it follows that in no part of natural philosophy can the production of the world be examined. Because such production is not natural, it does not fall within the scope of the science of nature.

Boethius notes that it also follows from this that the natural philosopher cannot show that there was a first man. While nature can produce something only through generation, the first man could not have been generated. Boethius's point again seems to be that if there was a first man, he had to be created. But, as we have just seen, the principles of natural philosophy do not extend to creation.

Central to Boethius's reasoning until this point is his view that the specialist in a given science must reason solely according to the principles of that science.[27] To bring in factors which do not follow

---

[27] See below, pp. 46-50. We shall see Boethius appealing to this principle again in his treatise *On Dreams*. For references to his usage of it in other works see Pinborg, "Zur Philosophie des Boethius de Dacia," pp. 170-172, 176-177; Sajó, *Introduction* to his edition of Boethius's *De Generatione et Corruptione* (Corpus Philosophorum Danicorum Medii Aevi, 5.1), pp. xxv-xxvi (for parallel citations from Boethius's *De modis significandi* and his *Quaestiones super libros Topicorum*).

from the principles of that science would be to violate its integrity. Still, as Boethius himself observes, one may object to him that it is true according to Christian faith and true in the absolute sense that the world did begin to be, that creation is possible, that there was a first man, and that given the doctrine of resurrection of the body, the dead will return as numerically one and the same without being generated a second time and those who have been raised from the dead will then be incorruptible. If the natural philosopher cannot establish or even know any of these truths from his principles, he should not deny them.

In reply Boethius counters that the natural philosopher should not deny truths which do not follow from the principles of his science if such truths are not contrary to the principles of his science and do not destroy that science. Thus if the natural philosopher cannot prove certain mathematical truths from the principles of his own science, he should not deny them since they are not opposed to the principles of natural philosophy. But, continues Boethius, the natural philosopher should deny any truth which he cannot know or prove from the principles of his science if that truth is opposed to the principles of his science and destroys it. If what follows from the principles of his science is to be granted, what is opposed to them is to be denied.

In light of this Boethius makes what at first sight appears to be a daring claim. The natural philosopher should deny that a dead man can immediately return to life, or that a thing which is subject to generation can be brought into being without being generated as is implied by Christian belief in resurrection. The natural philosopher should deny such truths because *qua* natural philosopher he should concede nothing which is not possible by reason of natural causes. The Christian rightly accepts them as true because, according to his religious belief, they are produced by a higher cause.

One may still object: If such claims are true, does not the natural philosopher speak falsely in denying them? In replying to this Boethius introduces the most subtle feature of his solution to the faith-reason problem. One can say that there was a first motion and that the world began to be, and yet that the world did not begin to be through natural causes and principles. In like fashion one can say both that the world and the first motion began to be, and that the natural philosopher speaks the truth when he denies that the world and the first motion began to be; for this is to deny that they began to be through natural causes and principles.

The reader will note how easy it would be to conclude from this that Boethius is saying that two contradictory propositions can be true at the same time and hence that he is defending a double-truth theory. In fact he is saying no such thing. His point is that when the natural philosopher denies that the world and the first motion began to be, he does so as a natural philosopher. The natural philosopher denies that this can be so according to natural causes and principles. If this denial is false when it is taken without qualification, it is in accord with the principles and arguments of natural philosophy.

As Boethius explains, the Christian speaks the truth and the absolute truth when he says that the world began to be, that there was a first man, and when in defending the resurrection of the body he holds that numerically one and the same man will return. Such truths are conceded to be possible because of the power of a cause which is greater than any natural cause. But the natural philosopher also speaks the truth when he says that such things are not possible from purely natural causes and principles. And, Boethius reminds us once again, the natural philosopher concedes or denies something only in terms of natural principles and causes. Therefore, Boethius insists, there is no contradiction between the natural philosopher who denies that such things are possible from natural causes and principles and Christian faith which, because it takes into account a higher cause and principle, asserts the opposite. Boethius sums up this long but important discussion by making two points: 1. regarding the eternity of the world the natural philosopher does not contradict Christian faith; 2. by purely natural argumentation it cannot be shown that the world began to be.

Boethius next turns to mathematics in order to show that the mathematician is likewise unable to prove that the world began to be. He divides mathematics into four parts, astronomy, geometry, arithmetic and music, and argues that none of these parts can establish this point. He devotes most of his attention to the first two parts of mathematics. Astronomy itself may be subdivided into a part which teaches about the motions and speeds of the heavenly bodies and their different positions, etc., and another part which deals with the effects which the stars have on the lower world. But the conclusions of astronomy in both of its parts will be the same whether the world began to be or whether the world is eternal. Geometry cannot prove that the world began to be because the principles of geometry, and therefore its conclusions, will hold whether or not the world is eternal. The metaphysician is likewise unable to prove that the world began to be. The world depends upon the divine will as upon its sufficient cause. But, reasons Boethius, the metaphysician cannot demonstrate that an effect can follow after its sufficient cause in duration. In other words, once a sufficient cause is posited for a given effect, including all the conditions required for that sufficient cause to act, the metaphysician cannot show that the effect can be delayed, as it were, so as to come after its sufficient cause in duration. Moreover, the metaphysician cannot demonstrate that it was the intention of the divine will from eternity to produce the world as something which began to be. Who would dare claim that any man, the metaphysician included, can know the eternal decrees of the divine will?

In sum, according to Boethius no philosopher can demonstrate that the world began to be. In defending this position, he is, of course, rejecting the claim advanced by many conservative theologians at Paris at that time, namely, that human reason can demonstrate that the world began to be. Bonaventure, John Pecham, and Henry of Ghent may be cited as leading advocates of that position, although it was defended by many others as well. And in denying that purely philosophical argumentation can prove that the world began to be, Boethius is also in agreement with Thomas Aquinas.[28]

[28] For an introduction to this thirteenth-century controversy about the possibility of demonstrating that the world began to be see F. Van Steenberghen, *Thomas Aquinas and Radical Aristotelianism* (Washington, D.C., 1980) pp. 1-27. It should be noted that on this particular issue Van Steenberghen sides with Bonaventure against the view defended by Thomas Aquinas. Also see Wippel, *The Metaphysical Thought of Godfrey of Fontaines: A Study in Late Thirteenth-Century Philosophy* (Washington, D.C., 1981), pp. 153-159. For additional discussion of particular features of Aquinas's position and further bibliography see Wippel, "Did Thomas Aquinas Defend the Possibility of an Eternally Created World? (The *De aeternitate mundi Revisited*)," *Journal of the History of Philosophy* 19 (1981), 21-37 (repr. in Wippel, *Metaphysical Themes in Thomas Aquinas* [Washington, D.C., 1984], Ch. 8); and J. Weisheipl, "The Date and Context of Aquinas' *De aeternitate mundi*," in *Graceful Reason: Essays in Ancient and Medieval Philosophy Presented to Joseph Owens, CSSR* (Toronto, 1983), pp. 239-271. Now see also L. Bianchi, *L'errore di Aristotele. La polemica contro l'eternità del mondo nel XIII secolo* (Florence, 1984), *passim*, and especially pp. 63-73 (on Boethius of Dacia).

It is equally important to note that Boethius denies that purely rational argumentation can prove that the world is eternal. To prove this one would have to demonstrate the intention of the divine will and this, Boethius insists, is beyond the capacity of any philosopher. Boethius reminds his reader that religious faith teaches many things which reason cannot demonstrate, for instance, resurrection of the body. Not to believe in such truths would be heretical, but to attempt to demonstrate them philosophically would be foolish.

Boethius's treatise concludes with a detailed discussion of and reply to the series of arguments he had presented to prove that the world is eternal. While limitations of space will not permit individual examination of these replies in this Introduction, they are strongly recommended to the reader. In them much of the thinking we have already seen recurs, along with a number of additional precisions regarding Boethius's philosophical outlook. As he reminds his reader after having replied to all of these arguments, the philosopher regards something as possible or as impossible for reasons which are open to rational investigation. While noting that philosophy does not rest on revelation or on miracles, Boethius insists that there is a place for faith as well.

Boethius is obviously satisfied that he has shown that there is a proper distinction between faith and reason, and that the two do not contradict one another either as regards eternity of the world or as regards other issues which can be held by faith alone. At the same time he has strongly defended the autonomy of philosophy. And by implication he has also introduced an interesting view concerning the degree of certainty which attaches to properly demonstrated conclusions in a particular philosophical science such as the philosophy of nature. While such correctly demonstrated conclusions necessarily and therefore truly follow from the principles of such a science, it may be that in a given case a higher power or cause intervenes so as to suspend, as it were, the application of these principles. Hence such correctly demonstrated conclusions would not then be true in the absolute sense.[29]

[29] One writer concludes from this that Boethius defends a relativistic view of the particular sciences. This is not to say that for Boethius truth itself is relative, but that the truth of the conclusions drawn in a particular science is relative to the application in a given situation of that science's principles. See P. Wilpert, "Boethius von Dacien — Die Autonomie des Philosophen," in *Miscellanea Mediaevalia* 3 (Berlin, 1964), 135-152, esp. 144, 150.

If it is clear that there is no defense of a double-truth theory in this treatise, it is also evident enough that either a careless or an unfriendly reader might think that such is to be found there. This may account for a reference to such a theory in the Prologue to Bishop Stephen Tempier's Condemnation in 1277.[30] Moreover, in the concluding part of his work Boethius reasserts the fundamental harmony between philosophy and religious faith. He then protests in rather indignant terms: "Why therefore do you grumble against the philosopher...?" A little farther on he adds: "...you should make a greater effort, because you have so little understanding of the philosophers who were and are the wise men of the world, to be capable of understanding their words." As if this were not enough, almost at the end of his treatise he comments that if someone, "whether enjoying a position of dignity or not, cannot understand such difficult matters, then let him obey the wise man and let him believe in the Christian law."[31] Such words were not likely to soothe the feelings of those to whom they were directed whether Boethius had in mind conservative theologians in the Faculty of Theology at Paris or whether, as seems to be implied by the last-mentioned remark, he also had in mind Bishop Stephen Tempier.

This brings us back to the Condemnation of 1277. As has already been mentioned, a number of the condemned articles are thought to have been taken from Boethius's treatise *On the Eternity of the World*. In discussing his *On the Supreme Good* we noted that article 154, while capturing something of the spirit of that treatise, seems to be directly aimed at Boethius's *On the Eternity of the World*.[32] According to the condemned proposition, *only* the philosophers are the wise men of this world. According to the present treatise, as we have just seen, the "philosophers were and are the wise men of the world." The word "only" does not appear in Boethius's text, and some hold that as that text reads, it contains nothing contrary to Christian orthodoxy. At least one recent writer rejects this interpretation, however,

---

[30] See *Chartularium* 1: 543: "For they say they are true according to philosophy but not according to the Catholic faith, as if there were two contrary truths, and as if the truth in the sayings of the accursed gentiles were contrary to the truth of sacred scripture."

[31] See below, pp. 65-67.

[32] See above, p. 9.

and argues that in fact even as the statement appears in Boethius's treatise it is objectionable; it leaves no place for a higher theological wisdom, even though it does allow for a wisdom which is not of this world, i.e., Christian faith. Hence, according to that writer, Tempier was right in condemning it.[33]

For other condemned propositions which seem to have been aimed at this treatise one should consider the following: article 145 (Mandonnet 6);[34] article 90 (Mandonnet 191): "That the natural philosopher should deny without qualification that the world began to be since he bases himself upon natural causes and natural arguments; but the believer can deny the eternity of the world because he bases himself upon supernatural causes;" article 25 (Mandonnet 214): "That God cannot grant perpetuity to a changeable and corruptible thing;" article 17 (Mandonnet 215): "That it does not happen that a corrupted body returns as numerically the same, nor will it arise as numerically the same;" article 18 (Mandonnet 216): "That a future resurrection should not be granted by the philosopher, because it is impossible for this to be investigated by reason. — This is an error because even the philosopher should make his intellect captive to the obedience of Christ."

For discussion of these and for the point that each bears a perfectly orthodox interpretation when taken in its original context within Boethius's *De aeternitate mundi*, see Hissette, *Enquête*.[35] It is important to note that in article 90 an all important term has been added which renders the proposition unacceptable from the standpoint of Christian orthodoxy, but which is missing from Boethius's text. The term, of course, is "without qualification" (*simpliciter*). Boethius's point is that the natural philosopher should deny that the world began to be according to natural causes and principles, that is, in a qualified sense (*secundum quid*) rather than without qualification (*simpliciter*). As regards the following three articles as they are listed in the preceding

---

[33] In defense of Boethius on this point see Hissette, *Enquête sur les 219 articles,* p. 19; Van Steenberghen, *Maître Siger*, p. 225, n. 9. For a much more critical evaluation concerning the same see Gauthier, "Notes sur Siger de Brabant," p. 19, n. 30. It seems to this writer that the omission of the term "only" from Boethius's text is more significant than Gauthier is willing to allow.

[34] This has already been discussed above. See pp. 10-11, and note 25.

[35] See pp. 284-285, 307, 308, 309.

paragraph, Boethius would defend each of them only with this same reservation — that they follow from natural causes and principles. He has refused to defend them in the unqualified sense. [36]

ON DREAMS

Boethius prefaces his discussion of dreams with a brief introductory section where he speaks of human actions, human goods, and the powers in man whereby he performs such actions and attains such goods. Of these powers some are natural, some are moral and some are intellectual; so too, therefore, are man's actions as well as the goods he achieves through such actions. In other words, of these goods some are natural, some are moral, and some are intellectual. Supreme among man's natural goods are the preservation of the individual and the continuation of the human species. Man's supreme moral good is political happiness. His supreme intellectual goods are knowledge and contemplation of truth and delight in the same. This final observation sets the stage for Boethius to take up the main issue to be considered in this treatise. Certain men of contemplation — philosophers, presumably — have wondered about the apparent absence of any cause to account for the knowledge of future events which seems to take place in dreams.

Boethius presents himself as writing this treatise in response to such queries. As he states the question: Is science through dreams possible? Or as he also puts it: Can one have foreknowledge of future events through dreams? In developing his answer to this central question, he will also offer a more general causal account of dreams. [37]

---

[36] For other propositions that may probably or at least possibly be directed against Boethius and even against his *De aeternitate mundi* see Hissette, *Enquête*, p. 314, n. 33, p. 315, nn. 36, 37.

[37] For a good overall discussion of this treatise see G. Fioravanti, "La 'scientia sompnialis' di Boezio di Dacia," *Atti della Accademia delle Scienze di Torino. Classe di Scienze morale* 101 (1966-1967), 329-369. While pointing out the obvious usage Boethius has made of Aristotle (pp. 341-345) in preparing this treatise, Fioravanti also stresses Boethius's concern to offer a strictly scientific account of dreams, including those which in some way indicate something about the future (pp. 362-369). Fioravanti contrasts Boethius's effort to arrive at an explanation of dreams in terms of their causes with the "more mystical or less naturalistic" explanations offered by Averroes and by Albert the Great (see p. 367).

In normal scholastic fashion Boethius first presents some arguments which would indicate that knowledge of the future through dreams is simply not possible. After three such arguments he offers another for the opposite side. There is hardly anyone who has not experienced this: after having a dream which indicates something about the future, he awakens and finds that the thing in question has come to pass.

In working out his own reply, Boethius begins by acknowledging that some kind of knowledge about the future is possible through dreams. He distinguishes between different kinds of dreams. Of these some are nothing but coincidental; they bear no relation to any future event beyond pure coincidence. Just as lightning sometimes flashes when someone is walking without there being any kind of causal connection between the lightning and the walking, so it is with such dreams. The event in question would have happened even if one had not dreamed about it. As for the cause of such dreams, they result from phantasms (images based on sense experience) which we have received when we were awake and which remain within the soul. When we have fallen asleep and our external activities have come to a halt and, for that matter, the motion of ascending vapors within us has also lost its force, such phantasms appear in the imagination. Such an appearance is a dream. Dreams of this kind — those which have nothing but a coincidental relationship with future events — are especially likely to deceive the dreamer. When one awakens one may see the actual thing whose phantasms had been preserved in his imagination. He may then conclude that it was because he dreamed about that thing that he now sees it in reality. Such, of course, is not the case, since there is no causal connection between his dream and his subsequent perception of that particular thing. In sum, such dreams tell us nothing about the future.

In contrast, Boethius notes that there is another kind of dream which does in some way cause future events. He observes that it may happen that if a person thinks deeply about something while he is sleeping, he will remember that thing when he awakens. In like manner it may happen that the phantasm of something he could possibly do appears to him in a dream, and while he is still sleeping he works out the proper way of doing it. Upon awakening he recalls his dream and judges that the course of action he had worked out while sleeping is appropriate and then proceeds to perform the action just as he had dreamed of doing. In some sense this kind of dream is a cause of the individual's future action because his recollection of the dream prompts him to perform the action. Hence Boethius suggests that in knowing such a dream one may also know the future event (by knowing its cause).

Boethius comments that other dreams are signs of future events.[38] Of these some are caused by an external agent as, for instance, by a heavenly body which alters the transparent medium to such an extent that it also affects the body of one who is asleep. As a consequence a greater or lesser degree of heat may be produced in the one who is sleeping. When his imagination perceives this, it forms an image which is appropriate for that particular passion which the sleeper is undergoing, and the sleeper dreams, for example, that he is walking through fire or some such thing. Or if it is rather a cooling process which is introduced into the body of the sleeper by some external cause, his imagination will note this and perhaps will also take into account another motion produced by another phantasm which had already been received in the soul. In such a case the imagination may form a composite image which combines a number of such things which are not united in reality. As a consequence the dreamer may dream that he is walking through snow, or some such thing.

It may be possible for the sleeper, once he has awakened, to identify the particular passion or reaction within his body from which his dream has followed. If so, this may enable him to discover the particular heavenly body which produced the original passion in him, or whatever that cause may have been. And because such a passion can cause some future effect in his own body, such as health or sickness, he may also be able to determine that certain effects will follow from his dream; for in reality they will follow from the passion in his body to which his dream corresponded.

At the same time, warns Boethius, such a passion may be impeded from producing its effect by some other factor. For instance, in matters of human choice, continuing reflection may lead one to follow a different course of action. So too, on the level of purely natural causes, a given cause may be prevented from producing its effect by a stronger cause. Consequently, when a natural philosopher draws

---

[38] See below, p. 72.

a conclusion from such causes — causes which can be impeded — he does not establish the conclusion in the unqualified sense but only as one which will follow from the natural causes if they are not impeded. Again we see Boethius appealing to his theory that a particular science must operate only in light of its own principles and causes, and his recognition that purely natural causes can be impeded from producing their effects.

Boethius comments that other dreams are caused by something within us rather than by something external. This internal factor may fall on the side of the soul or on the side of the body. As for dreams which are caused by something within us from the side of the body, he offers various illustrations. Different motions and combinations of fumes or vapors and the different rates at which they ascend to the imagination may lead a sleeper to dream, for instance, of flames and fires, or of black monks (Benedictines) and devils, or of angels singing and dancing, etc. Boethius hastens to add that while natural causes can account for such dreams, he does not intend to deny that by divine will an angel or devil can also really appear to one who is asleep or suffering from illness.[39] Boethius accounts for the different forms that dreams may take by appealing once more to the varying combinations and successions of the fumes and vapors which ascend to and move the imagination. This highly naturalistic and physiological explanation of dreams leads him to urge that the dreams of the ill should be made known to physicians. Through such dreams a skilled physician may be able to determine from what passions the sick are suffering, and what future effects are likely to follow from these passions if appropriate measures are not taken.

As for dreams produced in us from the side of the soul, Boethius comments that when a sleeper is subject to a strong passion such as fear or love, his imagination forms corresponding images. This may result in the phantasm of an enemy or of a beloved, about whom he then dreams. Upon awakening he should be able to identify the passion to which he had been subject and the future effects that passion may cause. Boethius concludes his treatise by appealing again to physiological explanations similar to those already mentioned

---

[39] See below, p. 75.

to account for the fact that dreams often do not occur in children and also, to explain why dreams of monsters do.

While Boethius is deeply indebted to earlier philosophers (especially to Aristotle and among his contemporaries to Thomas Aquinas) for much of his thinking in this treatise, his account is original and personal. One can hardly accuse him of indulging in any kind of superstition in his discussion of dreams. If dreams do take place, there are natural causes and explanations to account for them. If some dreams enable one to divine something about the future, this too ultimately can be explained through natural causes. For instance, someone may remember his dream upon awakening and that recollection will be enough for him to decide to carry out the particular action about which he had dreamed. Or the passion which caused a particular dream may be identified, and may also be recognized as being likely to cause some future effect within the body of the one who had dreamed. In fact, it seems that his account may have been too naturalistic and physiological for Stephen Tempier and his advisers. Thus article 33 (Mandonnet 177) from the list condemned in 1277 reads as follows: "That raptures and visions do not take place except through nature." It seems likely that Boethius's discussion in the present treatise was the source for this prohibited article.[40] Nonetheless, as already noted, Boethius has also allowed for divinely willed appearances of angels and devils in dreams. Once again, therefore, the prohibited article does not accurately reflect Boethius's position.[41]

The following translations are based on the recent edition of these three treatises by N. G. Green-Pedersen.[42]

---

[40] For discussion of this see Hissette, *Enquête*, pp. 271-272. Cf. Fioravanti, "La 'scientia sompnialis'," p. 331.

[41] As Hissette notes, this is not surprising, since this is only one of many instances in which Stephen Tempier's commission failed to read with sufficient care the texts with which they were concerned (p. 272, n. 8).

[42] See n. 1 above.

Boethius of Dacia

On the Supreme Good

On the Eternity
of the World

On Dreams

On the Supreme Good[1]

Since in every kind of being there is a supreme possible good, and since man too is a certain kind [*lit.* species] of being, there must be a supreme possible good for man. I do not speak of a good which is supreme in the absolute sense, but of one that is supreme for man; for the goods which are accessible to man are limited and do not extend to infinity. By reason let us seek to determine what the supreme good is which is accessible to man.

The supreme good for man should be his in terms of his highest power, and not according to the vegetative soul, which is [also] found in plants, nor according to the sensitive soul, which is [also] found in animals and from which their sensual pleasures arise. But man's highest power is his reason and intellect. For this is the supreme director of human life both in the order of speculation and in the order of action. Therefore, the supreme good attainable by man must be his by means of his intellect. Therefore, men who are so weighed down by sense pleasures that they lose intellectual goods should grieve. For they never attain their supreme good. They are so given to the senses that they do not seek that which is the good of the intellect itself. Against these the Philosopher protests, saying: "Woe to you men who are numbered among beasts and who do not attend

---

[1] Also edited by M. Grabmann, in "Die Opuscula De Summo Bono sive De Vita Philosophi und De Sompniis des Boetius von Dacien," *Mittelalterliches Geistesleben* 2 (1936), 200-224. For the Latin text see pp. 209-216. My earlier translation of this work was based on that edition. It is reprinted here in revised form with permission of the Free Press, a Division of Macmillan, Inc. from *Medieval Philosophy: From St. Augustine to Nicholas of Cusa*, edited by John F. Wippel and Allan B. Wolter, OFM. Copyright © 1969 by the Free Press. The present revised version is based on the improved Green-Pedersen edition. For this see *Boethii Daci Opera... Opuscula*, Corpus Philosophorum Danicorum Medii Aevi, 6.2 (Copenhagen, 1976), pp. 367-377.

to that which is divine within you!''[2] He calls the intellect that which is divine in man. For if there is anything divine in man, it is right for it to be the intellect. Just as that which is best among all beings is the divine, so also that which is best in man we call divine.

Moreover, one power of the human intellect is speculative and the other practical. This is clear from this fact, that man theorizes about certain objects which he does not actively cause, e.g., eternal things, and actively causes others under the intellect's direction whereby he realizes a means which can be chosen in human acts. From this, then, we know in general that these two intellectual powers are present in man.[3] But the supreme good accessible to man in terms of the speculative power of his intellect is knowledge of what is true and delight in the same. Knowledge of what is true gives delight. An intelligible object gives delight to the one who knows it. And the more wondrous and noble the intelligible object and the greater the power of the apprehending intellect to comprehend perfectly, the greater the intellectual delight. One who has tasted such delight spurns every lesser pleasure, such as that of sense. The latter is, in truth, less, and is more base. And the man who chooses such pleasure is, because of that pleasure, more base than one who chooses the former.

It is because of this, because the object known gives delight to the one who knows, that the Philosopher [Aristotle] in Book 12 of the *Metaphysics* maintains that the first intellect enjoys the most pleasurable life.[4] For since the first intellect is the most powerful in

---

[2] Neither Grabmann nor Green-Pedersen has succeeded in finding this passage in Aristotle; nor have I.

[3] Cf. Aristotle, *Metaphysics* 6, c. 1 (1025b 18-28), for the distinction between theoretical, productive, and practical thought and, corresponding to this, sciences. As used there and as Boethius here uses the term "speculative," it is captured in English by contemplation which is sought for its own sake.

[4] Note that Green-Pedersen follows another manuscript tradition and reads this as Book 11 of the *Metaphysics* (p. 370:42). If this is indeed the original reading, it would suggest a date prior to 1270, the widely accepted date for William of Moerbeke's revision of the Latin translation of Aristotle's *Metaphysics*, which included his translation of Book 11. This meant, of course, that Bk 12, by our numbering, had until then been known as Bk 11. On this see J. Weisheipl, *Friar Thomas d'Aquino. His Life, Thought and Works*, With *Corrigenda* and *Addenda* (Washington, D.C., 1983), pp. 235, 474. For Aristotle see *Metaphysics* 12, c. 7 (1072b 24).

understanding and the object which it knows is the noblest, its essence itself — for what nobler object can the divine intellect have than the divine essence? — therefore, it has the life of greatest delight. No greater good can befall man in terms of his speculative intellect than knowledge of the totality of beings which come from the first principle and, by means of this, knowledge of the first principle insofar as such is possible, and delight in it. Therefore, our conclusion above follows: that the supreme good available to man by means of his speculative intellect is knowledge of what is true in individual cases, and delight in the same.

Likewise, the supreme good available to man in terms of his practical intellect is the doing of good, and delight in the same. For what greater good can befall man in terms of his practical intellect than to realize a fitting means in human action and to delight therein?

No man is just save him who takes delight in acts of justice. The same must be said of the acts of the other moral virtues. From what has been said one can evidently conclude that the supreme good open to man is to know the true, to do the good, and to delight in both.

And because the highest good possible for man is happiness, it follows that human happiness consists in knowing the true, doing the good, and taking delight in both. The military profession is prescribed in a state by the lawmaker for this reason, that when enemies have been expelled, citizens may devote themselves to intellectual virtues in contemplating the true, and to moral virtues in doing good, and thus live a happy life; for the happy life consists in these two.[5] This then is a greater good, which man can receive from God and which God can give to man in this life. With reason does a man desire a long life who desires it for this, to become more perfect in this good. He who shares more perfectly in that happiness which reason tells us is possible for man in this life draws closer to that happiness which we expect in the life to come on the authority of faith.[6]

And since so great a good is possible for man, as has been said, it is right for all human actions to be directed toward that good, so

[5] Cf. Aristotle, *Nic. Ethics* 10, c. 7 (1177b 4-1178a 8); Thomas Aquinas, *In 10 Ethic.*, lect. 11 (Leonine ed., Vol. 47.2, pp. 586-588).

[6] As mentioned above in the Introduction (p. 6), this is the single reference in this work to religious belief in a greater happiness in the life to come.

as to attain it. All actions regarding a certain law are right and proper when they tend toward the end of the law, and better the more closely they approach the end of the law. Actions which are opposed to the end of the law or which are weak (and not perfect according to the precepts of the law)[7] or even indifferent (without either being opposed to the end of the law or in accord with its precepts), all such actions are sin against that law to a greater or lesser degree as is clear from what has been said. The same is true in man himself. All designs and deliberations, all actions and desires of man which tend to this supreme good which is available to man according to the above, these are right and proper. When man so acts, he acts in accord with nature. For he acts for the sake of the supreme good, to which he is ordered by nature. And when he so acts he is properly ordered, for then he is ordered to his best and his ultimate end. But all actions of man which are not ordered to this good, or which are not such as to render man stronger and better disposed for actions which are ordered to this good, all such actions in man are sin.

Wherefore the happy man never does anything except works of happiness, or works by means of which he becomes stronger and better fitted for works of happiness. Therefore, whether the happy man sleeps or is awake or is eating, he lives in happiness so long as he does those things in order to be rendered stronger for the works of happiness. Therefore, all acts of man which are not directed to this supreme good of man which has been described, whether they are opposed to it or whether they are indifferent, all such acts constitute sin in man to a greater or lesser degree, as is clear.[8] The cause of all such acts is inordinate desire. It is also the cause of all moral evil. Moreover, inordinate desire in man is the cause which most greatly prevents him from attaining that which is desired naturally. For all men naturally desire to know.[9] But only the smallest number of men, sad to say, devote themselves to the pursuit of wisdom. Inordinate desire bars the others from such a good. Thus we find

---

[7] The words in parenthesis (''and...law'') are missing from the Grabmann edition (see p. 211:24), and therefore from my earlier translation.

[8] Here, as in the preceding paragraph, Boethius rejects the possibility that human actions, i.e., those for which man is responsible, might be regarded as morally indifferent.

[9] See the opening words of Aristotle's *Metaphysics*, 1, c. 1 (980a 21).

certain men pursuing a life of laziness, others detestable sense pleasures, and others giving themselves to the desire for riches. So it is that all today are prevented by inordinate desire from attaining to their supreme good, with the exception of a very small number of men, men who should be honored.

I say they are to be honored because they despise sense desire and pursue the delight of reason and intellectual desire, laboring after[10] knowledge of the truth of things. Again I say they are to be honored because they live according to the natural order. All lower powers found in man naturally are for the sake of the highest power. Thus the nutritive power is there for the sake of the sensitive. For the sensitive power is a perfection of an animated body, and an animated body cannot live without food. But it is the nutritive power which changes and assimilates food. Therefore, it follows that the nutritive power exists in man for the sake of the sensitive. And the sensitive power is for the sake of the intellective since, in us, intelligibles are derived from things imagined. Wherefore, we understand with greater difficulty things which of themselves cannot be imagined by us. But imagination presupposes the senses. The proof of this is that one who imagines is also affected on the level of sense. Wherefore, according to the Philisopher, imagination or *phantasia* is a movement arising from an actual exercise of sense.[11] [Just as all lower powers in man are for the sake of the highest], so too the operations of all man's lower powers are for the sake of the operations of his highest power, the intellect. And if, among the operations of the intellective power, there is one which is best and most perfect, all others naturally exist for its sake. When a man performs such an operation, he enjoys the highest state possible for man.

Such men are the philosophers, who spend their lives in the pursuit of wisdom. Wherefore, all powers found in the philosopher operate according to the natural order, the prior for the sake of the posterior, the lower for the sake of the higher and more perfect. But all other men, who live according to lower powers and choose their operations

---

[10] Literally: "sweating after."

[11] See Aristotle, *De anima* 3, c. 3 (429a 1-2). On imagination as distinct both from perception (by the external senses) and from thinking see earlier in this same chapter (427b 14-428b 30).

and the pleasures found in such operations, are not ordered in accord with nature. They sin against the natural order. For man to turn away from the natural order is sin in man. Because the philosopher does not turn away from this order, for this reason he does not sin against the natural order.

Morally speaking, the philosopher is virtuous for three reasons. *First*, because he recognizes the baseness of action in which vice consists and the nobility of action in which virtue consists. Therefore, he can more easily choose the one and avoid the other and always act according to right reason. He who so acts never sins. But such is not true of the ignorant man. It is difficult for him to act rightly. *Secondly*, because he who has tasted a greater delight despises every lesser delight. But the philosopher has tasted intellectual delight in theoretical consideration of the truths of beings. This delight is greater than that of sense. Therefore, he despises sense pleasures. But many sins and vices consist in excessive sense pleasure. *Thirdly*, because there is no sin in understanding and theorizing. There is no possibility of excess and of sin in the order of absolute goods. But the action of the philosopher is such a contemplation of truth. Therefore, it is easier for the philosopher to be virtuous than for another. [12]

So it is that the philosopher lives as man was born to live, and according to the natural order. Since in man all lower powers and their operations are for the sake of higher powers and their operations, and all taken together for the highest power and that highest action, which is contemplation of truth and delight in the same, above all, the first truth, the desire to know will never be satisfied until the

---

[12] One might wonder whether Boethius has not here fallen into the position attributed to Socrates to the effect that virtue is knowledge. Because the philosopher understands the baseness of vice and the nobility of virtuous action, because he has tasted the highest kind of pleasure — theoretical contemplation, and because there can be no excess in the pursuit of absolute goods, the philosopher must be virtuous. Yet Boethius does not quite draw this conclusion. He rather claims that because of these things it is easier for the philosopher to be virtuous than for others; he can more easily choose virtue and avoid vice. The purely natural character of Boethius's argument is evident, since there is no appeal to the need for grace. But this is to be expected, in light of the purely philosophical character of the treatise.

uncreated being is known. As the Commentator says, all men naturally desire to know about the divine intellect.[13]

Desire for any knowable object is a kind of desire for the first knowable object. This is the proof. The closer beings are to the first knowable being, the more we desire to know them and the more we delight in thinking of them. Therefore, by studying the caused beings which are in the world and their natures and relationships to one another, the philosopher is led to consider the highest causes of things. For a knowledge of effects leads to a knowledge of the cause. And in noting that higher causes and their natures are such that they must have another cause, he is led to a knowledge of the first cause.[14] And because there is pleasure in speculative knowledge, and all the more so the nobler the objects known, the philosopher leads a life of very great pleasure.

The philosopher also knows and observes that it is necessary for this cause to be its own cause of being, that is to say, not to have another cause. If there were nothing in the universe which was not caused by another, then there would be nothing at all. He also notes that this cause must be eternal and unchangeable, always remaining the same. For if it were not eternal, then nothing whatsoever would be eternal. And again, since certain things in the world have begun to be, and since one being which begins to be cannot be a sufficient cause of another being which begins to be, as is evident, it clearly

---

[13] See *In XII Met.*, com. 51, in *Aristotelis opera cum Averrois commentariis*, Vol. 8 (Venice, 1562), f. 335r.

[14] According to one recent writer, there is tension between the claim made by Boethius in the preceding paragraph ("the desire to know will never be satisfied until the uncreated being is known") and the kind of knowledge of God Boethius in fact allows to the philosopher — that of a cause discovered by reasoning from its effects. It would seem that such discursive knowledge will never be enough to satisfy our desire to know God, and that only a direct intuitive knowledge of the divine essence will do so. See G. Wieland, *Ethica — Scientia practica*, p. 216. In Boethius's defense it may be noted that such a tension is to be expected in a purely philosophical discussion of man's desire for perfect knowledge and perfect happiness. Some such tension is also present in Aquinas's thought, but he, of course, can appeal as a believing Christian and as a theologian to religious belief in grace and in the beatific vision in coming to terms with it. For a nuanced discussion of Aquinas's solution see J. Laporta, *La destinée de la nature humaine selon Thomas d'Aquin* (Paris, 1965), passim. Also see J. Owens, *Human Destiny* (Washington, D.C., 1985), ch. 2.

follows that all things in this world which begin to be must derive from an eternal cause. This cause is also unchangeable and always remains the same, for change is possible only in imperfect things. And if there is some most perfect being in the universe, it is right for this to be the first cause.

The philosopher also notes that the entire being of the universe, with the exception of this first cause itself, must come from it and thus, just as this first cause is the cause which produces beings, so it orders them to one another and maintains them in existence — certain ones in terms of their individual identity and without any kind of change (as the separated substances); certain ones according to their individual identity, but as subject to change (as the heavenly bodies); and certain ones in terms of their species alone (as those which are below the sphere of [the moon] such as the lowest levels of beings). [15]

He also notes that just as all things derive from this first cause, so too, all things are ordered to it. For that being in which the principle from which all things [come] is joined to the end to which all things [return], [16] that is the first being according to the philosophers and God the Blessed according to the holy men. Nevertheless, in this order there is great range. Those beings which are closest to the first principle are nobler and more perfect. Those things which are farther removed from the first principle are lower and less perfect.

This first principle is to this world as the father of a family is to his household, as a commander is to his army, and as the common good is to the state. Just as the army is one because of the unity of its commander, and just as the good of the army is in the commander essentially and in others according to their relationship to him, so too, from the unity of this first principle derives the unity of the

---

[15] For Boethius the First Cause is not merely an unmoved mover but that which both produces and conserves its effects in terms of their being. According to the prevailing view of his time, Boethius would not admit that heavenly bodies are subject to corruption, but that they do undergo change by way of circular motion. Bodies which fall below the lunar sphere — earthly bodies — are subject to generation and corruption.

[16] Here the Green-Pedersen text is much clearer than Grabmann's reading: "Nam ens illud, in quo est principium, a quo omnia coniunguntur illi fini, ad quem omnia..." (*op. cit.*, p. 215:20-21).

world, and the good of this world is in this first principle essentially, and in other beings of this world insofar as they participate in the first principle and are ordered to it. So it is that there is no good in any being in this world which is not participated from the first principle.

Considering all these things, the philosopher is moved to wonder at this first principle and to love it. For we love that from which our goods derive, and we love that to the greatest degree from which our greatest goods derive.

Therefore, the philosopher, noting that all goods come to him from this first principle and are preserved for him insofar as they are preserved by this first principle, is moved to the greatest love for this first principle. This is in accord with the right order of nature[17] and with right reason from the side of the intellect. And since everyone takes delight in that which he loves and maximum delight in that which he loves to the maximum degree, and since the philosopher has the greatest love for this first principle, as has been indicated, it follows that the philosopher takes maximum delight in this first principle and in contemplating its goodness, and that this alone is right pleasure. This is the life of the philosopher. Whoever does not lead such a life does not live rightly. However, I call "philosopher" any man who lives according to the right order of nature and who has acquired the best and ultimate end of human life. And the first principle of whom we have spoken is the glorious and most high God, who is blessed forever and ever. Amen.

---

[17] Reading "right order" of nature with manuscript G (Paris, Bibliothèque Nationale 15.819), which contains a very early abbreviation of this treatise and which was part of the library belonging to Godfrey of Fontaines and left by him to the Sorbonne. This is significant since Godfrey was a student at Paris during part of Boethius's regency there, and quite likely in the Arts Faculty for some of that time. Godfrey went on to study theology at Paris and served as Regent Master in Theology from 1285 until ca. 1298 or 1299, and then again ca. 1303/1304. Godfrey's interest in the thought of Siger of Brabant and of Boethius of Dacia is amply attested to by the presence of a number of their works in his personal library. See Wippel, *The Metaphysical Thought of Godfrey of Fontaines. A Study in Late Thirteenth-Century Philosophy* (Washington, D.C., 1981), pp. xvi-xix.

On the Eternity of the World

Just as it is foolish to seek rational argumentation for things which should be believed by reason of the Law[1] and which admit of no such argumentation (for one who does so seeks that which cannot be found), and since it is heretical to refuse to believe such things without rational argumentation, so too it is unphilosophical to wish to believe without rational support things which are not self-evident but which do admit of rational argumentation in their support.

Therefore, it is our wish to bring into harmony the view of Christian faith concerning the eternity of the world and the view of Aristotle and of certain other philosophers. — [First of all], so that faith's position may be firmly maintained even though in certain cases it cannot be demonstrated, lest otherwise we fall into foolishness by seeking demonstration where such is not possible, or into heresy by refusing to believe that which should be held on faith and which cannot be demonstrated (as did certain philosophers for whom no revealed law was acceptable because the articles of such a revealed law did not admit of demonstration). — [Again], so that the position of the philosophers may be maintained to the extent that their argumentation is conclusive (for their position in no way contradicts Christian faith, except in the eyes of those who lack understanding. For the view of the philosophers rests on demonstrations and on other possible arguments in those matters whereof they speak, but in many instances faith rests on miracles and not on rational arguments. But that which is held because it follows from rational arguments is not faith but science.) — [And finally], so that it may be clear that faith

---

[1] The term "Law" as it is used here refers to a religion based on a scriptural revelation, and was a fairly common way of identifying the same in medieval Latin translations of Islamic and Jewish thinkers. It is reflected in Latin writers such as Albert the Great, Thomas Aquinas, and especially in Masters in the Faculty of Arts at Paris. Hence it could be applied to any of the three great religions based on scriptures — Judaism, Islam, and Christianity.

and philosophy do not contradict one another with respect to the
eternity of the world and also, that it may be evident that the arguments
of certain heretics whereby they maintain against Christian faith that
the world is eternal have no force. Let us, therefore, investigate this
question by reason, namely, whether the world is eternal.[2]

It seems that the world is not eternal.

1. The first principle is the cause of the substance of the world
since, if it were not, there would be many first principles. But that
which has being from another comes after that thing in duration.
Therefore the world comes after the first principle in duration. But
an eternal being comes after nothing in duration. Therefore, the world
is not eternal.[3]

2. Likewise, nothing can be equal to God. If therefore the world
were eternal, the world would be equal to God in duration. But this
is impossible.

3. Likewise, a finite power cannot produce an infinite duration,
since duration does not exceed the power which produces it. But the
power of the heaven is finite, as is the power of any finite body.
Therefore, the power of the heaven cannot produce an eternal duration.
Therefore, the heaven is not eternal. Therefore, neither is the whole
world, since the world is not prior to the heaven.

4. Likewise, God is prior to the world in nature. But in God
nature and duration are one and the same. Therefore God is prior to
the world in duration. Therefore the world is not eternal.

5. Likewise, every created thing was made from nothing. Creation
and generation differ in this, because all generation proceeds from

---

[2] Throughout this treatise Boethius is using the term ''eternity'' simply to express
the view that the world did not begin to be, not that such a world, if it did exist
without beginning, would enjoy divine eternity, i.e., the ''whole, simultaneous and
perfect possession of unending life,'' as the other Boethius had defined this in his
Consolation of Philosophy 5, pr. 6 (*Boethius. The Theological Tractates. The Consolation
of Philosophy*, tr. by S. J. Tester [Cambridge, Mass., 1978], p. 422). Boethius of
Dacia's usage is in accord with the prevailing practice of his time and with that of
earlier discussions of this issue in Greek, Arabic and Jewish philosophy.

[3] The point that if the world receives its being from another (God), then it must
come into being after its cause has existed appears frequently among arguments to
prove that the world began to be. For a classical statement of this see St. Bonaventure,
In II Sent., d. 1, p. 1, a. 1, q. 2, in *Doctoris Seraphici S. Bonaventurae... Opera
Omnia*, 10 Vols. (Quaracchi, 1882-1902), 2: 22.

a subject and from matter. Therefore, one who generates does not have power over the entire substance of the thing [produced]. But creation does not proceed from a subject and from matter. Therefore, one who creates has power over the total substance of the thing [created]. But the world was created since before the world there was no subject and no matter from which the world might be made. Therefore the world is from nothing. But such [to be from nothing] implies being after there was nonbeing.[4] Since, therefore, being and nonbeing could not be simultaneous, there was first nonbeing and afterwards being. But that which has being after nonbeing began to be. Therefore the world began to be. Therefore it is not eternal since to begin to be and to be eternal are mutually exclusive for one and the same thing.

6. Also, there can be something greater than that which admits of addition. But time can be added to all the time that has gone before. Therefore, there can be something greater than the total time that has gone before. But nothing can be greater than the infinite. Therefore, the totality of time that has gone before is not infinite. Therefore neither is motion and neither is the world.

7. Again, if the world were eternal the generation of animals and of plants and of simple bodies would be eternal. Therefore a given individual would result from an infinity of generating causes, because if generation were eternal, then this individual instance of man would precede that one, and still another that one, and so on to infinity. But it is impossible for one effect to result from an infinity of agent causes; for if there is no first agent or mover there is no motion, since the first mover is the cause of the total motion, as is written in Bk 2 of the *Metaphysics*,[5] and as is self-evident. There can be no first within an infinity of agents. Therefore this generation [that of animals, plants, and simple bodies] is not eternal. Therefore neither is the world.

8. Likewise, Aristotle maintains in Bk 6 of the *Physics*[6] that as regards finiteness and infinity the same holds for magnitude, motion, and time. Therefore since no magnitude is infinite, as Aristotle proves

---

[4] See note 3 above.

[5] *Metaphysics* 2, c. 2 (994a 18-19).

[6] *Physics* 6, c. 1 (231b 18-20).

in Bk 3 of the *Physics*,[7] neither is motion infinite nor is time. Therefore neither is the world since the world does not exist without these.

9.   Likewise, if the world were eternal an infinity of men would have been generated and corrupted. But when a man is corrupted that substance which was in his body remains, that is, his rational soul, since it is not subject to generation and corruption. Thus such substances would be simultaneously infinite in act. But it is impossible for an infinity of things to exist in act simultaneously. Therefore, etc.

10.   Again, if the world were eternal an infinite motion would have been passed through as well as an infinite time because, if the world were eternal, the time prior to this instant would be infinite. But it is impossible for the infinite to be passed through and to be completed. Therefore etc.[8]

11.   Again, that which has a distinct cause has a beginning. The world has a distinct cause: "For the sea was made because the world was made," as is said in Bk 2 of the treatise *On Meteors*.[9] Therefore the world has a beginning. But what has a beginning is not eternal. Therefore, etc.

For the contrary position it is argued, first, that the world *can be* eternal and that nothing impossible follows from this; secondly, it is shown that the world *is* eternal.[10]

1.   The first point is established in this way. Although an effect follows after its cause in the order of nature, it can nonetheless be

---

[7] *Physics* 3, c. 6 (206a 16).

[8] There is similarity between some of the arguments presented here and others offered by Bonaventure in his Commentary on *II Sent.* as cited above in note 3. See pp. 20-22. For an English translation of the latter see *St. Thomas Aquinas, Siger of Brabant, St. Bonaventure: On the Eternity of the World*, tr. by C. Vollert, L. H. Kendzierski, P. M. Byrne (Milwaukee, 1964), pp. 107-109.

[9] *Meteora* 2, c. 3 (356b 4-7).

[10] As Boethius's organization of this question shows, it is one thing to claim that the world *can be* eternal; it is something else again to claim that the world *is* eternal. As is well known, Thomas Aquinas consistently maintained throughout his career that human reason has not demonstrated that the world began to be, and in at least some texts, including his earliest discussion, that human reason cannot do so. Only in his very late treatment in the *De aeternitate mundi* (ca. 1270) did he go so far as to claim that an eternally created world is possible, at least according to my interpretation of this. See my "Thomas Aquinas on the Possibility of Eternal Creation," Ch. 8 in *Metaphysical Themes in Thomas Aquinas* (Washington, D.C., 1984), pp. 191-214.

simultaneous with its cause in duration. The world as well as every caused being is an effect of the first being. Therefore, since the first being is eternal, the world can be coeternal with it. The major is evident because things which are prior and posterior in terms of nature may be simultaneous in terms of duration.[11] The minor is also evident because, just as in any genus the first must be the cause of everything else, so too in the genus of being the first being must be the cause of all other beings. From this it follows that the first being is an uncaused being because it must be the sufficient cause of [all other] things. But no caused thing is the sufficient cause for any of its effects since all of its effects depend upon that same thing upon which the essence of the caused being depends. Therefore the first being must be a being which has no other cause. Otherwise it would not be the first being.

2.   This same point is clear from Aristotle's statement in *Physics* 8 that even if something is eternal it need not be a principle. For a triangle to have three angles equal to two right angles is eternally the case, but another cause must be sought to account for this eternal situation.[12] Therefore that which is eternal can be caused. Since, therefore, nothing can be prior in duration to that which is eternal, an effect can be coeternal with its cause. The world is the effect of the first being. Therefore the world can be coeternal with it.

3.   Again, an example will make this point clear. If the sun were always in our hemisphere, light would always be present in the [transparent] medium, and light would be coeternal with the sun and nonetheless its effect. This would not be so unless it were possible for an effect to be simultaneous with its cause in duration.

4.   Again, if a foot were always embedded in dust, its print would be coeternal with it and nonetheless its effect.[13]

5.   Again, this same point may be established by the following argument. Nothing is eternal in the future without a past, since the power which can make the duration of something eternal in the future

---

[11] Literally: "The major is evident because priority and posteriority in nature and simultaneity in duration are compatible with one another."

[12] *Physics* 8, c. 1 (252b 2-4).

[13] Thomas Aquinas uses this same example in his *De aeternitate mundi* (Leonine ed., 43: 88) and explicitly takes it from Augustine's *De civitate Dei* 10, c. 31 (Corpus Christianorum, Series Latina, 47: 309).

can also have made its duration eternal in the past; for such a power is unchangeable and always conducts itself in the same way. But the world is eternal as regards the future both according to the view of Christian faith and according to the opinion of certain philosophers. Therefore by reason of the same power [which can make the world eternal as regards the future], it [the world] could have been eternal with respect to the past.

Thus, therefore, the world *can be* eternal, and from such a suggestion no impossibility seems to follow from the side of reason, nor from this can any untoward consequence be established by argumentation. And this will be clear to anyone who directs his attention to this matter.

The following argumentation is offered to show that the world *is* eternal.

1. Everything which is incorruptible has the capability of existing always; for if it did not have such a capability, it would not be incorruptible. But the world is incorruptible since what is not generated is incorruptible. Therefore the world has the capability of existing always. But a thing exists throughout the entire duration to which its ability to exist extends. Therefore, the world is eternal.

2. Likewise, that is eternal which admits of no duration before itself. Everything which begins to be has some duration before itself. But the world had no duration before itself because there was no time. There was no time before the world since time follows upon the motion of the first mobile even as a *passio* follows upon its subject. Nor was there eternity before the world, because that which is preceded by an eternal duration never exists. If, therefore, before the world there was eternal duration, the world would have never existed.

3. Likewise, that which is made *de novo* can be made. If this were not so, then that which cannot be made would be made. But that by reason of which a thing can be made is matter. But before the production of the world there was no matter from which the world could be made. Therefore, the world was not made with a temporal beginning. Therefore, the world is eternal, since there is no intermediary between that which begins to be and that which is eternal.[14]

---

[14] There is an interesting similarity between this argument and one presented by Aquinas in *Summa theologiae 1*, qu. 46, art. 1, arg. 2.

4. Again, everything which begins to be is produced through change, since to eliminate change is to eliminate every beginning. But every change requires a subject and matter, as is written at the beginning of *Metaphysics* 8 and in *Metaphysics* 7, and in *Physics* 3: "that motion and every change is the act of a being in potency insofar as it is in potency." [15] Since, therefore, before the world there was no matter and no subject of change which would be required for the world to be newly made if the world were something newly made, the world is not something newly made but is eternal.

5. Again, that which begins to be exists in time, since that which begins in any duration must come to be within a part of that duration. That which occurs during an entire day does not begin to be on that day. That which takes place during an entire year does not begin to be in that year. Rather that which begins to be within the year must occur during some part of that year. But of all durations time alone has parts. The world is not prior to time. Therefore the world is not something which began to be but is eternal.

6. Likewise, every process of generation proceeds from something which is corrupted, and everything which is corrupted was previously generated. In like manner, every instance of corruption proceeds from something which was generated, and everything generated arises from something corrupted. Therefore, before every generation there is generation, and before every corruption there is corruption. Therefore there should be no first generation or first corruption. Therefore generation and corruption are eternal. Therefore the world is eternal, since those things which are generated and corrupted are parts of the world and cannot be prior to the world in duration.

7. Likewise, an effect cannot follow after its sufficient cause in duration. The sufficient cause of the world is eternal because it is the first principle. Therefore the world cannot follow after it in duration. Therefore the world is coeternal with it. And this argument is confirmed as follows. A being which is eternal both in terms of its substance and in terms of its every disposition, to which nothing is added in the future and from which nothing is lacking in the past of that whereby it would produce its effect, produces its immediate

---

[15] See Aristotle, *Metaphysics* 8, c. 1 (1042a 32-34); *Metaphysics* 7, c. 7 (1032a 17-20); *Physics* 3, c. 1 (201a 10-11).

effect as coeternal to itself. God is an eternal being both in terms of his substance and in terms of every disposition present in him, to whom nothing is added in the future and from whom nothing is lacking in the past of that whereby he would produce his effect. And the world is his immediate effect. Therefore the world is coeternal with God.

8.   Likewise, Aristotle says in *Metaphysics* 9[16] that, as regards an agent which acts by its will, when it can act and wills to act, then it acts. Nor is it necessary to add "if there is no impediment," since the term "can" eliminates any impediment. But from eternity God had the power and the will to produce the world. Therefore the world is an eternal effect.

9.   Likewise, every effect which begins to be requires something new in one of its principles; for if all of the principles for a given effect always remained exactly the same, from them no effect could be produced when it had not previously existed. But there can be nothing new in the principle for the world, which is the first being. Therefore the world is not an effect which began to be. And this argument is confirmed. A given agent, if it itself has begun to be in terms of its substance, can be the cause of a new effect; or [an agent can be the cause of a new effect] if it is eternal in terms of its substance but has begun to be with respect to some power or some position (as is clear in the case of a heavenly body); or if it was previously subject to some impediment; or if some new disposition has been introduced into the subject on which it acts. In the cause of the world none of these is possible, as is self-evident. Therefore the world is not an effect which began to be.

10.   Again, everything which is in motion after having been at rest is traced back to a continuous motion which always is; for something to be in motion at one time and to be at rest at another cannot be owing to an immobile cause. Since it is not possible to regress to infinity in motions each of which is the cause of another, it is therefore necessary for the first motion to be continuous and eternal. For this reason in *Physics* 8[17] Aristotle traces back every motion which begins to be to a first motion as to its cause, which

[16] See *Metaphysics* 9, c. 5 (1048a 13-20).
[17] See *Physics* 8, c. 5 (256a 8ff.).

[motion] according to Aristotle's view is eternal. And Aristotle holds this view for this reason: a motion which always has its sufficient causes cannot begin to be. But the first motion always has its sufficient causes since, if this were not so, another motion would have been prior to it, by which sufficiency would have been produced in its causes after having been lacking to them. Therefore it would be first and not first, which is impossible.

11. Again, a will which postpones that which it wills awaits something in the future. Before the world there was no awaiting because before the world there was no time, and awaiting occurs only in time. Therefore the world was not postponed after the divine will. But the divine will is eternal. Therefore the world is coeternal with the divine will.

12. Again, every effect which depends upon some will as upon its sufficient cause (between which effect and that will no duration transpires) is simultaneous with that will; for those things are simultaneous in duration between which no duration transpires. But the world depends upon the divine will as upon its sufficient cause — for it has no other cause — and between these no duration transpires because there is neither time (for before the world there was no time) nor eternity (because then the nonexistence of the world would take place in eternity. Since, therefore, that which takes place in eternity is eternal, then the nonexistence of the world would be eternal. Therefore the world would never be, which is impossible). Therefore the world is coeternal with the divine will.

13. Again, every effect which begins to be must be preceded by some kind of change, either in its agent, or in the subject from which it is made, or at least that [change] which is the coming of the moment (*hora*) in which the agent, without itself undergoing change, wills to act. Before the world there could be no change. Therefore the world cannot be an effect which began to be.

Someone may counter that nonetheless the world is an effect which began to be because this was the intention (lit. form) of the divine will from eternity, to produce the world in that moment in which it was made. A new effect can proceed from an old will and for this reason it is unnecessary for there to be any change either in the will or in the one who wills. Thus someone now may have the will of doing something after three days. When the third day arrives he then does that which he had previously willed and of old, without there being any change in the will or in the one who wills. And in this way the world can have a beginning even though it has an eternal sufficient cause.

Against this line of reasoning it is argued as follows. He who imagines the antecedent imagines all that follows from it, but does not prove it. You imagine that in God there is such an intention of will from eternity, but you cannot prove it. In such fashion it is easy to imagine anything. Someone will say to you that the intention of the divine will was not such from eternity, and you will have no basis on which to contradict him. Therefore you also imagine that the world began to be, but you are unable to prove it.

Again, against this way of reasoning there is the following argument. What is willed proceeds from the will according to the intention of the will. If such therefore was the intention of the divine will that from eternity it willed to produce the world at [this] moment, as you say, then it would have been impossible for God to have produced the world previously. This seems to be unfitting since God is an agent who acts through freedom of will.

To this argument you will reply that, nay, God could have produced the world previously because just as he had this intention of will from eternity, so he could have had another and, therefore, just as he produced the world at the moment in which it was made, he could have produced it previously.

But against this reasoning there is this argument. What has one form of will and can have another is changeable as regards wills. But God is completely unchangeable. Therefore he cannot have a form of will different from that which he has had from eternity.

Again, a new effect cannot be made from an old will if there is no change between it [the will] and its effect. What accounts for the fact that an effect is not simultaneous in duration with its cause is the change that occurs between them. To take away such change is to take away all awaiting. But there can be no change between God's will, which is eternal, and the world. Therefore, before the world there can be no change. Therefore the world is coeternal with the divine will.

Again, as regards the example which has been proposed, it is not to the point, that is, that someone now has the will of doing something after three days, and when the third day arrives he does that which he has willed from of old. The example is not to the point because, while there was no change in the will or in the one willing, nonetheless there was that change which is the coming of the moment, that is, of the third day. But if there were no change in the one who wills, nor in a passive subject from which the new effect should be made, nor that change which is the coming of the moment, then a new effect could not be produced from an old willing; for every new effect requires some change before itself, as someone would say. And because before the world there was no change in the will from which the world was made, nor in the matter from which the world should be made — because matter did not exist before the world — nor before the world was there that change which is the coming of some moment, then it seems that a new world could not be made from an eternal will. And therefore the example is not to the point.

These are the arguments by which certain heretics who defend the eternity of the world attempt to attack the position of Christian faith which holds that the world began to be. Against these arguments it is expedient for the Christian to work diligently so as to know how to resolve them perfectly, should any heretic raise them.

SOLUTION

First of all, it must be carefully noted here that there can be no question which may be disputed by rational arguments which the philosopher should not dispute and determine concerning where its truth lies, insofar as this can be grasped by human reason.[18] And the reason for this is that all the arguments by which such is disputed

---

[18] Cf. proposition 145 (Mandonnet, article 6) condemned by Bishop Stephen Tempier, 7 March, 1277 (quoted above in the *Introduction*, p. 11, n. 25). For similar reasoning see Boethius's *Quaestiones super libros Physicorum*, ed. by G. Sajó, Corpus Philosophorum Danicorum Medii Aevi, Vol. 5.2 (Copenhagen, 1974), Bk 1, qu. 2a, pp. 140, qu. 2b, 141-142. Note that in that same context Boethius asks whether apart from the philosophical disciplines any other science is necessary (qu. 1a, pp. 139-140). He replies that some, i.e., the ancient philosophers, maintained that no other sciences are necessary; for natural philosophy, metaphysics and mathematics cover the threefold division of being into natural, divine and mathematical. But, he continues, this position is not correct. There are other sciences which teach truths which are not accessible to philosophical inquiry, such as the science of the "modern, i.e., Christian Law" (see qu. 1b, p. 141). In other words, he clearly leaves a place for theology.

are taken from things. Otherwise they would be figments of the mind. But the philosopher teaches the natures of all things. For just as philosophy teaches of being, so do the parts of philosophy teach of the parts of being, as is written in *Metaphysics* 4,[19] and as is evident of itself. Therefore it belongs to the philosopher to determine every question which can be disputed by reason; for every question which can be disputed by rational arguments falls within some part of being. But the philosopher investigates all being — natural, mathematical, and divine. Therefore it belongs to the philosopher to determine every question which can be disputed by rational arguments. Let him who asserts the contrary know that he is ignorant of his own speech.

Secondly, it must be noted that neither the natural philosopher nor the mathematician nor the metaphysician can show by rational arguments that the first motion and the world began to be.

That the natural philosopher cannot establish this may be shown as follows, by accepting two self-evident presuppositions. The first of these is this, that one skilled in a given science can prove [lit. cause], concede, or deny something only in terms of the principles of his own science. The second is this, that although nature is not the first principle in the absolute sense, nonetheless it is the first principle in the realm of natural things, and the first principle which the natural philosopher can consider. And therefore, because Aristotle was aware of this in the *Physics*, which is the first book of the science of natural things, he began not from the first principle in the absolute sense but from the first principle for natural things, that is, from prime matter, which in Bk 2 of the *Physics* he says is nature.[20]

To apply these presuppositions to our point —

Nature cannot cause any new motion unless another motion which is its cause precedes it. But no other motion can be prior to the first motion, for then it would not be the first motion. Therefore, the natural philosopher, whose first principle is nature, cannot hold according to his principles that the first motion began to be. The major is evident since material nature produces nothing new unless it is first acted upon by another. For material nature cannot be the first mover. How will something which is generated be the first mover?

---

[19] See *Metaphysics* 4, c. 2 (1004a 2-9).
[20] See *Physics* 1, cc. 7-9; *Physics* 2, c. 1 (193a 28-30).

And every material agent is a being which is generated. Nor should one argue from the body of the heaven. If it is a material being, nonetheless, it does not have matter univocally with things subject to generation; for those things which share in matter of the same kind can be changed into one another.[21]

Likewise, every new natural effect requires some newness in its immediate principles. But newness cannot be present in any being without some prior change. To eliminate change is to eliminate all novelty. Therefore nature can cause no new motion or effect without some preceding change. Therefore, according to the natural philosopher, whose first principle is nature, the first motion, which can be preceded by no change, cannot begin to be. The major is evident because, if all the immediate principles for some natural effect were always disposed in the same way, that effect could not now result from them when it did not do so previously. I will ask why now rather than before, and you will have no way of replying. In this argument I speak of "immediate principles," because even when a natural effect is new, it need not follow from this that there is any change or

---

[21] Along with his contemporaries, Boethius accepts the Aristotelian view that heavenly bodies are not subject to generation and corruption. But in light of Aristotle's theory of matter-form composition of material entities, this poses a problem. If heavenly bodies are composed of matter and form, will they not be subject to corruption? Thomas Aquinas concluded that there are two different kinds of prime matter. The kind present in terrestial bodies carries with it the capacity to undergo corruption. Another kind of matter is present in heavenly bodies. This matter is ordered to a form which is so perfect and universal that any capacity for it to be ordered to another form is excluded. Therefore such a matter-form composite (heavenly body) is incorruptible. See, for instance, *Summa contra gentiles* 2, c. 98; *Summa theologiae* 1, qu. 84, art. 3, ad 1; *In De Caelo*, lect. 6. For full discussion see T. Litt, *Les corps célestes dans l'univers de saint Thomas d'Aquin* (Louvain-Paris, 1963), pp. 54-79. Boethius rather cautiously maintains here that if a heavenly body is a material being, its matter is not the same in kind as that of things subject to generation; for things which share in the same kind of matter can be changed into one another. For the same see his *Quaestiones de Generatione et Corruptione*, ed. by G. Sajó, Corpus Philosophorum Danicorum Medii Aevi, 5.1 (Copenhagen, 1972), 2, qu. 7, pp. 115-117. Because he was convinced that there cannot be two kinds of pure potentiality or prime matter, a few years later Godfrey of Fontaines proposed another solution as probable — there is no prime matter in the proper sense in a heavenly body (see his Quodlibet 5, qu. 2; Quodlibet 9, qu. 7). See Wippel, *The Metaphysical Thought of Godfrey of Fontaines* (Washington, D.C., 1981), pp. 285-291.

novelty in its mediate and first principles. Although the proximate principles of things which are capable of being generated are themselves changed and at times exist and at times do not exist, their first causes always exist.

From this it is clearly evident that the natural philosopher cannot posit any new motion unless some motion precedes it and is its cause. Therefore, since it is necessary to posit some first motion in the world — for there is no regress to infinity in motions each of which is the cause of another — it follows that the natural philosopher, from his science and its principles which he uses, cannot hold that there is a first motion which began to be.

Therefore in Bk 8 of the *Physics*, while inquiring whether motion came into being at some time after having previously not existed, and using these principles which have now been stated, Aristotle, speaking as a natural philosopher, concludes that the first motion is eternal, and this from both sides. [22] In the same Bk 8 of the *Physics* [23] he also inquires why certain things are sometimes at motion and sometimes at rest. He replies that this is because they are moved by a mover that is itself always moved. Because the mover whereby they are moved is a moved mover — and therefore exists under different dispositions — for this reason it makes the things it moves move on some occasions and rest on others. But those things which are always moved, such as heavenly bodies, are moved by an unmoved mover, which is always disposed in the same way [both] in itself and with respect to the things it moves.

If therefore the natural philosopher cannot in light of his principles posit a first motion which has begun to be, neither can he establish the existence of a first mobile thing [which has begun to be]; for a mobile thing is prior to its motion in the order of causality, since it is a kind of cause with respect to the same. Neither, therefore, can the natural philosopher show that the world began to be, since the first mobile thing is not prior to the world in terms of duration.

From this it clearly follows, if anyone carefully considers what we have already said, that the natural philosopher is unable to consider

---

[22] That is to say, both as regards the past and as regards the future. The first motion always was and always will be. See *Physics* 8, c. 1 (250b 11-252b 6).

[23] *Physics* 8, c. 6 (260a 11-19).

creation. For nature produces its every effect from a subject and from matter. But production from a subject and from matter is generation, not creation. Therefore the natural philosopher is unable to study creation.[24] How could the natural philosopher study something to which his principles do not extend? And since the making of the world or its production in being cannot be generation, as is evident, but is creation, from this it follows that in no part of natural science will the making of the world or its production in being be taught; for that production is not natural and therefore does not pertain to the natural philosopher.

From the above it also follows that the natural philosopher in his science is unable to show that there was a first man. The reason for this is as follows. Nature, about which the natural philosopher studies, can produce nothing except by way of generation, while the first man cannot be generated. Man and the sun generate man. The manner whereby the first man came into being is different from generation.[25] Nor should anyone be surprised that the natural philosopher is unable to consider those things to which the principles of his science do not extend. What has been said will appear reasonable to anyone who carefully considers those things which the natural philosopher as such can study. Not every practitioner [of science] can examine every truth.

You may object that it is true according to Christian faith and true without qualification that the world began to be and is not eternal, that creation is possible, that there was a first man, that a man who has died will return as living and as numerically the same and this without being generated,[26] that numerically the same man who was previously corruptible will be incorruptible and thus that in one indivisible (lit. atomic) species there will be these two differences,

---

[24] To create, of course, is to produce something from nothing, that is, from no preexisting subject. Boethius's point is that because the natural philosopher studies mobile being, he cannot take into account a kind of production which does not require a preexisting subject.

[25] Boethius's point is that the first man could have been produced only through creation. Boethius does not entertain the possibility of the evolution of man at some point in time from some lower species of animal.

[26] This is entailed by Christian belief in resurrection of the dead, whether as recorded in Scripture (see the raising of Lazarus) or at the end of time.

the corruptible and the incorruptible.[27] Even though the natural philosopher cannot establish these truths or even know them since the principles of his science do not extend to such difficult and hidden workings of divine wisdom, still he should not deny these truths. Although the practitioner of one science cannot demonstrate or know from his principles the truths of sciences practised by others, nonetheless he should not deny them. Therefore, although the natural philosopher can neither know nor assert the aforementioned truths by reason of his principles since the principles of his science do not extend to them, still he should not deny them if another proposes them as true not because of rational argumentation but because of a revelation effected by some higher cause.

To this it must be said that the natural philosopher should not deny those truths which he can neither establish nor know from his own principles if they are not contrary to his principles and do not destroy his science. Thus from his own principles the natural philosopher cannot prove it to be true that "there are four possible right angles surrounding any designated point on a surface." Nonetheless he should not deny this since it is neither contrary to his principles nor does it destroy his science. But he should deny any truth which he can neither establish nor know from his principles if it is contrary to his principles and destroys his science; for just as that which follows from his principles is to be conceded, that which is opposed to them is to be denied. Therefore, because the natural philosopher concedes nothing which he does not regard as possible by means of natural causes, he should deny that a dead man can immediately return to life, and that a generable thing can be brought into being without being generated — as the Christian holds who defends resurrection of the dead, as well he should, and [who believes] that the corrupted will return as numerically one and the same. But the Christian

---

[27] If Christian belief in the resurrection of all at the end of time is accepted, this seems to imply that within one and the same species there will have been corruptible individuals, and will then be incorruptible human beings. Note that one of the thirteen propositions condemned by Bishop Stephen Tempier in 1270 reads: "That God cannot endow a corruptible or mortal thing with the gift of immortality or incorruption." For these propositions see *Chartularium Universitatis Parisiensis* 1: 486-487, English translation in J. F. Wippel/A. B. Wolter, *Medieval Philosophy: From St. Augustine to Nicholas of Cusa* (New York, 1969), p. 366.

grants that these things are possible by reason of a higher cause which is the cause of the whole of nature. Therefore they do not contradict one another in these matters, just as they do not in others.

But you may also object, since it is the truth that ''a dead man immediately returns as alive and as numerically one and the same,'' as the Christian faith which is most true in its articles of belief holds, does not the natural philosopher who denies this say something false?

To this it must be said that just as one can say both that there was a first motion and that the world began to be and yet that the world did not begin to be through natural causes and principles, so too one can say, if he carefully considers the situation, both that the world and the first motion began to be and that the natural philosopher speaks the truth when he denies that the world and the first motion began to be.[28] This is so because the natural philosopher denies *as* a natural philosopher that the world and the first motion began to be, and this is for him to deny that the world began to be from natural principles. Whatever the natural philosopher denies or concedes *as* natural philosopher, this he denies or concedes from natural causes and principles. Wherefore the conclusion wherein the natural philosopher asserts that the world and the first motion did [not] begin to be is false when it is taken without qualification; but if it is referred back to the arguments and principles from which the natural philosopher derives it, it follows from these. For we know that both he who says that Socrates is white, and he who denies that Socrates is white in certain respects, speak the truth.

Thus the Christian speaks the truth when he says that the world and the first motion began to be, and that there was a first man, and that a man will return as living and as numerically one and the same, and that a generable thing can be produced without being generated; for such things are conceded to be possible by reason of a cause whose power is greater than that of any natural cause. The natural

---

[28] If one were to stop reading at this point, one could easily conclude that Boethius is defending the double-truth theory, i.e., that he is holding that two contradictory propositions can be true at the same time. That this is not his intent is clear from what follows. See our *Introduction*, pp. 4, n. 11, and 14. Bishop Stephen Tempier seems to have thought that such a theory was implied by a position very close to that defended here by Boethius. See the Prologue to the Condemnation of 1277 as cited in note 30 above of our *Introduction*. See *Chartularium* 1: 543.

philosopher also speaks the truth when he says that such things are not possible from natural causes and principles; for he concedes or denies something only from natural principles and causes, just as the grammarian denies or concedes something *as* grammarian only from grammatical principles and causes. And because the natural philosopher, in taking into account only the powers of natural causes, concludes that the world and the first motion did not begin[29] to be from these, while Christian faith, by taking into account a cause which is higher than nature, holds that the world could begin to be because of that [cause], the two do not contradict one another in any way. Thus two things are clear. The first is that the natural philosopher does not contradict Christian faith concerning the eternity of the world. The second is that by natural argumentation it cannot be shown that the world and the first motion began to be.

That the mathematician is unable to establish this may be shown as follows.[30] One part of mathematics is astronomy [*astrologia*], and this in turn is divided into two parts. One part teaches about the different motions of the stars and their speeds, which complete their course more quickly or more slowly, and their distances and conjunctions and appearances and other things of this kind. The other part of the science of the stars is that which teaches about the effects which the stars have on the entire body which is below the sphere. Neither those things which the first part [of astronomy] teaches nor those which the second part teaches show that the world and the first motion began to be. There can be such slownesses or quicknesses

---

[29] According to the *abbreviatio* of this treatise contained in Godfrey of Fontaines' library, this should rather read "could not begin to be." As the editor notes, this may well be the correct reading (see *ed. cit.*, p. 353, variant for line 486). For a transcription of the entire abbreviated version in Godfrey's text (Paris, Bibliothèque Nationale lat. 15819) see pp. 435-442. Cf. note 17 above to *On the Supreme Good*, p. 35. The editor also believes that this transcription, along with that of the *De summo bono* contained in the same manuscript, is in Godfrey's hand. See *Introduction*, p. vii.

[30] In accord with a widespread practice at the time, Boethius includes the quadrivium under one part of theoretical or speculative philosophy — mathematics. The quadrivium included arithmetic, geometry, astronomy, and music, and Boethius will now attempt to show that none of these can prove that the world and the first motion began to be. On various ways in which the sciences were classified during the medieval period see J. A. Weisheipl, "The Nature, Scope, and Classification of the Sciences," in *Science in the Middle Ages*, ed. D. C. Lindberg (Chicago, 1978), pp. 461-482.

of certain stars in their spheres with respect to other stars and also such conjunctions of them with one another even if the world and the first motion were eternal. For the same reason, neither can the second part of the science of the stars show that the world and the first motion began to be. By reason of the fact that the stars could have the same motions and conjunctions and powers which they now have even if the world and the first motion were eternal, they could also produce effects in the lower world similar to those which they now produce, even if the world and the first motion were eternal. Therefore neither can the second part of the science of the stars show that the first motion and the world began to be.

Just as the first part of the mathematical sciences is unable to establish this, neither can that part which is geometry. This does not follow from the principles of geometry since the opposite of the consequent can stand with the antecedent — that is to say, "that the first motion and the world are eternal" can stand with the principles of geometry and all its conclusions. If this false claim be granted that the first motion and the world are eternal, will it follow from this that the principles of geometry are false — such as that "a straight line runs from point to point," or that "a point is that which has no parts" and others like them? Or will its conclusions also be false? Clearly not. Will all the properties in magnitude be demonstrable in the same way of their subjects and through the same causes even if the world were eternal just as if the world began to be? Clearly so.

And I say the same about the third and the fourth parts of the mathematical sciences — arithmetic and music — and in the same manner as has been stated with respect to geometry. And this is evident to him who has advanced in these sciences and who is aware of their capabilities.

That the metaphysician is likewise unable to show that the world began to be is evident from the following. The world depends upon the divine will as upon its sufficient cause. But the metaphysician is unable to demonstrate that any effect can follow after its sufficient cause in duration, or can be postponed [to come] after its sufficient cause. Therefore the metaphysician cannot demonstrate that the world is [not] coeternal with the divine will.

Again, he who is unable to demonstrate that this was the intention (lit. form) of the divine will — that from eternity it willed to produce the world at the moment in which it was made — likewise cannot demonstrate that the world began to be and that it is not coeternal with the divine will. For that which is willed proceeds from the one who wills according to the intention of the will. But the metaphysician cannot demonstrate that such was the intention of the divine will from eternity. To say that the metaphysician could demonstrate this is not only like a figment [of the imagination] but is, in my opinion, akin to madness. From whence does this reasoning come to man, by which he might perfectly investigate the divine will?[31]

From all that has been said a syllogism may be formed. There is no question whose conclusion can be established by reason which the philosopher should not dispute and determine insofar as such is possible to reason, as has been stated.[32] But by reason no philosopher can show that the first motion and the world began to be, since such is not possible for the natural philosopher or for the mathematician or for the divine philosopher, as is evident from the above. Therefore, through no human argumentation can the first motion and the world be proved to have begun to be. Nor can it be shown that they are eternal, since he who would demonstrate this would have to demonstrate the intention of the divine will, and who will investigate this?[33] Therefore, Aristotle says in the *Topics* that "there is a kind of problem concerning which we hold an opinion for neither side, such as whether the world is eternal or not."[34] There are many things in the faith

---

[31] Here one is reminded of a remark made by Siger of Brabant in a question where he is attempting to determine whether or not the (separate) intellect is eternal or created *de novo*: "He who would know whether the intellect was produced *de novo* or as eternal must investigate the intention (lit. form) of the will of the First Agent. But who is there who will investigate this?" See his *Quaestiones in Tertium de Anima, De anima intellectiva, De aeternitate mundi*, ed. B. Bazán (Louvain-Paris, 1972), *In Tertium De Anima*, qu. 2, p. 7.

[32] See above, p. 46, and note 18.

[33] See note 31 above.

[34] See *Topics* 1, c. 11 (104b 8, 12-17). Note that Thomas Aquinas, apparently following Moses Maimonides on this point, interpreted this passage in his earlier writings so as to imply that Aristotle may not have really intended to demonstrate the eternity of the world, but only that arguments offered by others against its eternity were not demonstrative. See for instance, *In II Sent.*, d. 1, q. 1, a. 5, Mandonnet ed. (Paris, 1929), 2: 33-34. Late in his career Thomas rejected this reading of Aristotle and concluded that the Stagirite really thought that he had demonstrated the eternity of motion and hence of the world. See *In VIII Physic.*, lect. 2 (Turin and Rome,

which cannot be demonstrated by reason, as that the dead will return as living and as numerically the same, and that a generable thing will return without being generated. He who does not believe these things is a heretic; but he who seeks to establish them by reason is a fool.

Because, therefore, effects and works result from power, and power from substance, who dares say that he knows perfectly by reason [the divine substance and all of its power? Let him say that he knows perfectly] all of the immediate effects of God: how they derive from him whether by beginning to be or from eternity, and how they are preserved in being by him, and how they are present in him. For in him and from him and through him all things are made or are.[35] And who is there who can investigate this adequately? And because there are many things among those that faith professes which cannot be investigated by human reason, therefore, where reason falls short let faith supply, which ought to confess that divine power is beyond human understanding. Nor for this reason do you detract from the articles of faith because some of them cannot be demonstrated. If you proceed in such fashion you will stand under no law, since there is no law all of whose articles can be demonstrated.

Thus it is clearly evident that there is no contradiction between Christian faith and philosophy concerning the eternity of the world, if the above be carefully considered. With God's help we will establish the same about some other questions in which Christian faith and philosophy seem to disagree from a superficial point of view and to those who consider the matter without due care.

We maintain, therefore, that the world is not eternal but was created *de novo*, although this cannot be demonstrated by rational arguments, as we have seen above, as is also true of certain other

---

1954), n. 986, pp. 509-510. Cf. *In XII Metaphys.*, lect. 5 (Turin and Rome, 1950), nn. 2496-2497, p. 584. For Maimonides see his *The Guide of the Perplexed* (Chicago, 1963), 2, ch. 15, p. 292. For discussion see E. Behler, *Die Ewigkeit der Welt* (Munich, 1965), pp. 54-55, 260-261; J. Wippel, "Thomas Aquinas on the Possibility of Eternal Creation," Ch. 8 in *Metaphysical Themes in Thomas Aquinas*, p. 191; J. Weisheipl, "The Date and Context of Aquinas' *De Aeternitate Mundi*," in *Graceful Reason: Essays in Ancient and Medieval Philosophy Presented to Joseph Owens, CSSR*, ed. L. P. Gerson (Toronto, 1983), pp. 265-268.
[35] Cf. *Romans* 11, 36.

things which pertain to faith. If they could be demonstrated, then [faith] would not be faith but science. Therefore, in defense of the faith sophistical argumentation should not be advanced, as is evident; nor should dialectical argumentation, since it does not produce a firm habit but only opinion, and faith should be stronger than opinion; nor should demonstrative argumentation, since then faith would extend only to those things which can be demonstrated.

* * *

At this point it is necessary to reply to the arguments offered for both sides, and first to those which endeavor to prove that which is contrary to the truth, that is, that the world is coeternal with God. [36]

1. In reply to the first: "Everything which is incorruptible has the capability of existing always." By the term "incorruptible" you may understand that which when it exists cannot cease to be either by that corruption about which the Philosopher speaks at the end of *Physics* 1 [37] ("Everything which is corrupted will pass into this ultimate [subject], that is, into matter"), or by corruption taken more broadly than the Philosopher himself uses the term. This kind of corruption can happen to any being which is caused by something else, insofar as that being is viewed in itself. Any effect so long as it endures is conserved in being by some one of its causes, as is evident to the one who advances this argument. But that which is kept in being by something else can, insofar as it is in itself, cease to be. If the incorruptible is understood in both of these ways, then the major proposition is true which states: "everything which is incorruptible has the capability of existing always." [38] Taken in this way, therefore, the world is not incorruptible, nor is any being which is caused by something else.

---

[36] For these arguments see above, pp. 41-46. In fact Boethius will limit himself to refuting these arguments. He will not refute those which attempt to show that an eternal world is possible (see pp. 39-41), nor those which attempt to prove that the world began to be (see pp. 37-39).

[37] See *Physics* 1, c. 9 (192a 32ff.)

[38] The implication is that if something is not corruptible only in the narrower sense — by returning to its ultimate subject, or prime matter — the major premise will not hold. It will not follow from such incorruptibility that a thing has "the capability of existing always."

And you argue in proof: ''what is not generated is incorruptible.'' This is true of that corruption which is opposed to generation, because just as generation proceeds from matter, so does the corruption which is opposed to it proceed to matter, that is, to a contrary and not to a pure negation. But if something is not generated it is not necessary for this reason that it be incorruptible by corruption taken in the broader sense, that is, not into a contrary but into a pure negation. In this sense every caused being can be corrupted if the power of its conserving principle is withdrawn. The ancient philosophers referred to this kind of conservation as a golden chain whereby every being is conserved in its order by the first being; but the first being, having no cause prior to itself, has no conserving principle prior to itself.

And because this point has already been touched upon — that every being with the exception of the first is kept in being by the power of the first principle — let me explain this more fully.

And first of all through authority (lit. the statements of the authors). In the *Liber de causis* it is written: ''The fixing and the essence of every intelligence is [effected] by that pure goodness which is the first cause.''[39] By its essence he understands its production in being, and by its fixing he understands its duration. And if an intelligence endures by the power of the first principle, then all the more so do all other beings. And with this what is written in the Law agrees: ''From him and through him are all things.''[40]

Likewise, when speaking in the person of the first principle to the intelligences themselves, Plato says: ''My will is more important than your nature as regards maintaining your eternity.''[41]

The same point is shown by reason. A caused being does not have of itself a nature so as to exist because if it did have of itself a nature so as to exist, it would not be caused by another. But what endures and is kept in existence by its own power and not by another higher power has of itself a nature so as to exist. Therefore no caused being is preserved in existence by itself. And therefore just as all beings

---

[39] See *Liber de causis*, ed. by A. Pattin (Leuven, n.d./also published in *Tijdschrift voor Filosofie* 28 [1966], pp. 90-203), Prop. 8 (9), p. 66.

[40] See *Romans* 11, 36.

[41] See Plato, *Timaeus* 41B in *Plato Latinus IV: Timaeus a Calcidio translatus commentarioque instructus*, ed. J. H. Waszink (London-Leiden, 1975), p. 35: 15-17.

apart from the first principle derive from it, so too they are conserved in existence by it; and if the first principle should withdraw its power from these beings, [these] beings would not exist at all.[42] Thus it is written in the *Liber de causis*: "All dependent powers are from one first power which is the power of powers."[43] And in speaking about this first principle in his Commentary on *Metaphysics* 2 Averroes says: "that cause is nobler both in being and in truth than all beings; for all [other] beings do not acquire being and truth except from that cause. Therefore it is being itself through itself and true through itself, and all other beings are beings and true through its being and its truth."[44]

Likewise, the power which produces an eternal duration is itself an infinite power; for if it were finite, then a greater power could be realized. Therefore, since no duration can be greater than an eternal duration, it would follow that a greater power would not produce a greater duration than a lesser power, which is impossible. But in no caused being is there an infinite power, since every caused being is passed through or completely realized.[45] And this is repugnant to an infinite power.

---

[42] There can be no doubt, therefore, about Boethius's conviction that the First Being causes the existence of other beings and preserves or conserves them in existence. In other words, his First Being is not merely an unmoved mover. See our remark above to the same effect with respect to his *On the Supreme Good* (Introduction, p. 7).

[43] See *Liber de causis*, Prop. 15 (16), p. 80.

[44] See *In II Met.*, com. 4, in *Aristotelis opera cum Averrois commentariis*, Vol. 8 (Venice, 1562), f. 30r.

[45] Though there are some variant readings, this is the one preferred by Green-Pedersen and is that found in the manuscript in Godfrey of Fontaines' library (see p. 439). While Boethius's reasoning here is puzzling, this seems to be his point. Apparently guided by Aristotle's description of the infinite as that outside of which there is always something else (see *Physics* 3, c. 6 [207a 1ff], he accepts the general view of his time that the infinite cannot be passed through or traversed. (For reference to this by Aquinas see, for instance, Quodlibet 9, qu. 1; *Summa theologiae*, 1, q. 7, a. 4c). While this would be true of quantitative infinity for Aristotle, Thomas, and others, Boethius applies it in a metaphysical way, that is, to an effect insofar as it is an effect. As such, an effect must be passed through or traversed or "completely realized." By this he seems to mean that if it is an effect, it must be actually realized as such; it must exist completely, or not at all. And if it is so realized, it has been traversed, i.e., it is not that beyond which there is something more to be realized.

This same point is also proved in another way. Because the power of the first mover is greater than the power of any subsequent mover, and because nothing can be greater than the infinite, therefore infinite power and eternal duration belong to no caused being of itself, but only through the power of that first principle whose power is eternal and infinite of itself. And [this] argument may be stated as follows. Just as no duration can be realized which is greater than a duration which always is, so the power which produces a duration which always is or is eternal must be such that no power can be realized which is greater than it. Only an infinite power is such.

2.   In reply to the second argument. When you say, ''That is eternal which admits of no duration before itself,'' I counter that this is false. Although there is no time before the world, there is eternity before the world; for it [eternity] always is. You say: ''That which is preceded by an eternal duration never exists.'' I say that this is not necessarily the case. A new thing which was made today is preceded by an eternal duration because it is preceded by eternity itself which always is; nonetheless, it cannot be said that this [newly made thing] never exists.

3.   To the third argument it must be said that although a being which is produced from a subject and from matter or by generation depends upon a twofold potency, that is, on the active potency of its agent and on the potency of its matter — for nothing comes from matter except that to which matter itself is in passive potency — nonetheless those things which are not produced by generation or from matter depend only on the potency of their agent-principle, not on the potency of matter.[46] How can you say that something depends on the potency of matter if it is not itself produced from matter, as is true of the world? For it is evident to everyone that the world could not be produced by generation. Wherefore, if there were no

---

Therefore it is finite and cannot possess infinite power. In this argument Boethius seems to have shifted from extensive infinity (quantitative infinity) to intensive infinity. For his awareness of this distinction and his application of parallel reasoning to the infinite taken intensively see his *Quaestiones super libros Physicorum*, Bk 3, qu. 23b, p. 294: 79-82.

[46] For fuller discussion of these two usages of the term ''potency'' along with explicit acknowledgment of its roots in Aristotle's *Metaphysics* 5, c. 12, see Thomas Aquinas, *De potentia Dei*, q. 3, a. 14; *Summa contra gentiles* 2, c. 37. For discussion see Wippel, *Metaphysical Themes in Thomas Aquinas*, pp. 164-165.

other way of being made except generation, nothing whatsoever would have been made. Therefore I say that the world was made and was made *de novo*, because it is not coeternal with God. And when you say, "therefore it could be made," I say that this is true: it could be made only by the potency of its agent, not by reason of the potency of its subject and of matter. And because this point has already been touched on in the Solution — that an effect may depend on the power of its agent alone as upon its sufficient cause — about which someone might be in doubt, therefore this is explained as follows.

Everything which depends on matter in order to be made is impossible if there is no matter. The totality of being with the exception of the first principle was made, because all such being has a cause. By a being that is made I have in mind that which depends on another cause in order to be produced. If therefore every production depends upon matter and none depends solely upon the potency of an agent-principle, and if in addition to the totality of being which is distinct from the first principle there was not some matter, it follows that all being apart from the first principle would be impossible. Therefore something was made which cannot be made.

4. To the fourth argument this must be said. When you say "everything which begins to be is produced through change," this is true only of beings which are produced by generation. It is only in things subject to generation that change is found. Wherefore the heavenly bodies, which have substances which are not subject to generation, are generated in terms of their position just as they are changed in terms of their position.

5. In reply to the fifth argument, you say, "that which begins to be exists in time, since that which begins in any duration must come to be within a part of that duration;" for if it were simultaneous with every part of that duration it would not begin to be within that duration, and the only duration which has parts is time. To this I say that something can be said to begin to be in two ways — [in one way], because it exists after having previously not existed by having existence after its contradictory [i.e., nonexistence] without thereby implying that it is in one part of the duration in which it is but not in another part. It is in this way that the world began to be, and it is not necessary for such a thing which begins to be to be in time. In another way, something may be described as that which

begins to be because it enjoys existence in one part of the duration in which it is and nonexistence in another part of the same. What begins to be in this way necessarily exists in time because the only duration which has parts is time. And the world did not begin to be in this second way. Therefore the world could begin to be within no duration — neither in time, since the world began with time and hence no part of time is prior to the world; nor in eternity, because eternity is indivisible and what is in eternity always remains one and the same.

6.   To the sixth argument this must be said. When you say "Every process of generation proceeds from something which is corrupted," this is true. And when you say secondly, "Everything which is corrupted was previously generated," I say that the natural philosopher grants this proposition because in light of his principles he cannot maintain that a generable and corruptible thing can be made except through generation. He, however, who holds that a generable thing may be produced without being generated — as he should hold who posits a first man, since a man is a generable thing and his production cannot be by generation if he is the first — he should deny the proposition that "everything which is corrupted was previously generated;" for it contradicts his position. [47] The first man was corrupted at some point in time, even though he was never generated. Wherefore this sixth argument rests on natural principles; and it was stated above that he who holds that the world was newly made should set aside natural causes and seek for a higher cause.

7.   To the seventh argument this must be said. When you say that an effect cannot follow after its sufficient cause in duration, this is true of a cause which acts by nature, but not of [a cause] which acts in voluntary fashion. Just as God can know things which are new by his eternal intellect, although they are not new with respect to him, so by his eternal will he can produce new things.

8.   To the eighth argument this must be said. What can act and wills to act necessarily acts — this is true with respect to the moment to which the will is directed. Now, God's power is eternal, whereby he was capable of producing the world, and so is the will whereby he willed it. Nevertheless, because that will was concerned only with

[47] This is because he holds that the first man was created.

the moment in which the world was made, therefore the world is something which began to be even though God's will is eternal.

9. In reply to the other argument this must be said. When you say, "Every effect which begins to be requires something new in one of its principles," I say that this is not necessary in an agent which acts through will. According to an old will new actions can be produced without there being any change in the will or in the one who wills. In confirmation it must be said that not only can an agent produce a new effect because it has a new substance, or because it has some new power or position, or because it was previously subject to some impediment, or because a new disposition has been introduced into the passive principle on which it operates; but also some agent can produce a new effect because it has an eternal will directed to a given moment in which it wills to act according to that will.

10. To the following argument it must be said that it is not necessary for everything which is in motion after having been at rest to be traced back to an eternal motion; but it is necessary for everything which is in motion after having been at rest to be traced back to a first motion — as to a cause — which does not exist after having been at rest. Wherefore, although the first motion is new, it itself does not exist after having been at rest; for not every kind of immobility is rest, but rather the immobility of that whose nature it is to undergo motion, as is written in Bk 3 of the *Physics*. [48] And before the first motion there was no mobile thing whose nature it was to undergo motion (taking "before" in the sense of duration).

11. In reply to the next argument this must be said. You say, "A will which postpones that which it wills awaits something in the future." This is true only of that will whose action takes place in time; for only in time is there [any] coming of the future and awaiting. This is not true of a will whose action is before time. The action of the divine will is before time, at least that action whereby it was producing the world and time.

12. To the following argument it must be said that two things which are within the same duration are simultaneous if no part of that duration falls between them; thus two temporal beings are simultaneous in time if no part of time falls between them. However,

---

[48] See *Physics* 3, c. 2 (202a 3-5).

if no duration falls between the two for this reason that one is in the now of eternity and the other in the now of time (and hence no duration occurs between them), it does not necessarily follow that they are simultaneous. This is true of God's will, which is in the now of eternity, and of the production of the world, which is in the now of time.

13. To the next argument one must reply as was stated. You argue against this that to propose such an intention on the part of God's will is to indulge in idle imagination. It must be said that this is not true; for not all things which cannot be demonstrated are figments [of the imagination].[49]

To your second counterargument I say that since such was the intention of the divine will from eternity, such must have been the way in which that which was willed proceeded from the [divine] will, so that what is willed is perfectly conformed to the [divine] will.

To the other argument, when you say that a new effect cannot result from an old will if no change occurs between the will and its effect, this is true only of the kind of will from which an effect proceeds by change. The divine will is not of that kind.

To the other I say that the example is partly to the point, but not completely.

Let the arguments for the opposite side be granted for the sake of the conclusion, although they can be resolved, since they are sophistical.[50]

---

[49] In saying this, Boethius continues to leave a place for truths which can be accepted only on faith. Hence his position concerning this is far removed from one condemned by Bishop Stephen Tempier in 1277, to the effect that the statements of the theologian are based on fables (*Chartularium*, prop. 152/Mandonnet, prop. 183). For discussion of this proposition and three related ones see A. Maurer, "Siger of Brabant on Fables and Falsehoods in Religion," *Mediaeval Studies* 43 (1981), 515-530.

[50] See the arguments offered to prove that the world began to be (pp. 37-39). Given his efforts in the Solution of this treatise to show that the philosopher (whether natural philosopher, mathematician, or metaphysician) cannot prove that the world began to be, Boethius must regard all argumentation offered to demonstrate this conclusion as ineffectual or, as he puts it here, sophistical. It is interesting to note that he does not now judge it necessary to refute each of the particular arguments he had presented in support of this claim.

From all of this it is evident that for the philosopher to say that something is possible or impossible is to say that it is possible or impossible for reasons which can be investigated by man. When someone puts aside rational arguments, he immediately ceases to be a philosopher; philosophy does not rest on revelations and miracles. You yourself hold and ought to hold that many things are true, which, however, if you did not affirm them to be true except insofar as human reason could lead you to do so, you should never grant them. Such is true of the resurrection of men which faith teaches, and rightly so. In such matters one relies on divine authority, not on human reason. I will ask you what rational argument proves this. I will also ask what rational argument proves that a thing which is produced by generation can return again after its corruption without being generated, and even so as to be numerically the same as it was before its corruption. This must be the case in the resurrection of men according to the teaching of our faith. Nonetheless, at the end of *De Generatione* 2,[51] the Philosopher states that a corrupted thing can return again so as to be the same in species but not so as to be the same in number. In saying this he does not contradict the faith, because he says that this is not possible according to natural causes. The natural philosopher reasons from such causes. Our faith, however, teaches that this is possible by reason of a higher cause which is the beginning and the end of our faith, the glorious and blessed God.

Therefore there is no contradiction between faith and the philosopher. Why therefore do you grumble against the philosopher,[52] since you

---

[51] See *De Generatione et Corruptione* 2, c. 11 (338b 11-17).

[52] "Quare ergo murmuras contra philosophum...?" (*ed. cit.*, p. 365:826-827). Some later manuscripts of Thomas Aquinas's *De aeternitate mundi* add to its title the phrase *contra murmurantes* (see Leonine ed., Vol. 43, Introduction, p. 54). While there does not seem to be good authority for thinking that this was part of its original title, its presence in later manuscripts raises an interesting question concerning the precise target or targets Thomas had in mind when writing his treatise. For a recent examination of this see J. A. Weisheipl, "The Date and Context of Aquinas' *De aeternitate mundi*," in *Graceful Reason: Essays in Ancient and Medieval Philosophy Presented to Joseph Owens, CSSR*, ed. by L. P. Gerson (Toronto, 1983), pp. 239-271. Here Weisheipl comes to the conclusion that Thomas's treatise was not directed against any one theologian in particular, not even specifically Bonaventure or John Pecham, but against a widely prevailing view among Parisian theologians at least since the time of William of Auvergne to the effect that one can demonstrate that the

grant the same thing as he does? Nor should you think that the philosopher, who has devoted his life to the pursuit of wisdom, has contradicted the truth of the Catholic faith in any respect; but you should make a greater effort, because you have so little understanding of the philosophers who were and are the wise men of the world,[53] to be capable of understanding their words. The statement of a Master is to be given the best possible understanding; and what certain mean-spirited ones say who devote all of their efforts to this — to be able to find arguments which are in some way repugnant to Christian faith — is to no avail, and is undoubtedly impossible.[54] For they say that the Christian insofar as he is a Christian cannot be a philosopher because by reason of his Law he is compelled to destroy the principles of philosophy. This is false because the Christian grants that a conclusion derived from philosophical arguments cannot be otherwise by reason of those [principles] through which it has been reached. And if one concludes from natural causes that a dead man will not immediately return alive as numerically one and the same, the Christian concedes that this cannot be otherwise by reason of the natural causes through which the conclusion is reached; nonetheless, he concedes that this can be otherwise by reason of a higher cause which is the cause of the whole of nature and of all caused being. Therefore the Christian

---

world began to be (see pp. 270-271). Given the controversial climate at the time, one is tempted to seek for a particular target for Boethius's remark. In denying that noneternity of the world can be demonstrated, Boethius was certainly opposing the view held by the conservative majority in the Theology Faculty. In advancing his particular solution to the faith-reason problem he was at the least risking opposition from the same quarters, an opposition which would subsequently be expressed in the condemnation of a number of propositions by Bishop Stephen Tempier in 1277 (see our Introduction, pp. 17-19). See note 55 below.

[53] See the Condemnation of 1277, art. 154 (*Chartularium*)/art. 2 (Mandonnet). Cf. our Introduction, p. 17.

[54] As Boethius sees things, these "mean-spirited ones" (*maligni*) are giving anything but the best possible interpretation to the teachings of certain Masters (in Arts). Instead they are trying to pick out from what the Masters are saying (and writing, we may assume) arguments which are opposed to Christian belief. To report that Boethius or another Master holds that a dead person cannot return alive as numerically one and the same without adding the qualification "according to natural causes" would seem to be a good illustration of such a procedure. Boethius seems to have in mind certain students whom he accuses of such behavior, but we need not think that he is limiting his remark to students.

who understands deeply is not compelled by his Law to destroy the principles of philosophy, but preserves his faith and his philosophy by attacking neither.

If, however, someone, whether enjoying a position of dignity[55] or not, cannot understand such difficult matters, then let him obey the wise man and let him believe in the Christian Law — not because of sophistical argumentation which itself deceives; nor because of dialectical reasoning, for this does not produce so firm a habit as is faith since a conclusion from dialectical argumentation is held with fear of the opposite; nor because of demonstrative argumentation, both because such is not possible with respect to all the things which our Law holds, and also because it produces science — "demonstration is a syllogism which produces science," as is written in *Posterior Analytics* 1[56] — and faith is not science. May the author of this same Law, the glorious Christ who is God, blessed for ever and ever, make every Christian adhere to and believe this Law of Christ insofar as this is necessary. Amen.

---

[55] As I have suggested above in the Introduction (p. 17), here Boethius may have in mind Bishop Stephen Tempier, along with others. The Latin term *dignitas* ("in dignitate constitutus sive non") may mean an ecclesiastical benefice which includes the administration of ecclesiastical affairs together with the power of jurisdiction, a description which would apply to Stephen's office as Bishop of Paris, though the term has many other meanings as well. See Ch. DuCange, *Glossarium ad scriptores mediae et infimae latinitatis* (Paris, 1938), 3: 117.

[56] *Post. Analyt.* 1, c. 2 (71b 17-18).

On Dreams

Since every action is [performed] by some power and for some good, as for an agent's end, it follows that man's actions and the goods which are available to him from his actions must be distinguished in accord with the different kinds of powers which are present in him. Of the powers which are present in man, some are natural, some are moral, and some are intellectual. Accordingly, among man's actions certain ones are natural. The principle for such actions is not knowledge but nature. Others are moral. By these a man realizes a means which can be chosen in particular cases and which is determined according to the judgment of prudence. And others are contemplative actions. By these man investigates the truths of beings.

Because of this, also among the goods which are available for man, some are natural, some are moral, and others are intellectual. Supreme among natural goods is the preservation of the individual and the continuation of the species. It is for the sake of this that man does whatever he does naturally, that is, through his natural powers. These are the powers of nutrition and growth whereby the individual is preserved, and the power of generation whereby the species is continued. But the supreme good which is available to man from his moral actions is political happiness; for this is not for the sake of any other moral good, but rather all moral goods are for its sake. The ultimate good which is possible for man from his intellectual actions is a perfect knowledge of truth and contemplation of that truth, and the intellectual delight which is joined with such contemplation. This [delight] preserves the action of contemplation and continues it, since delight when joined to an action prolongs that action just as sorrow when joined to an action shortens and corrupts it. Those who seek other pleasures for themselves do this because they have tasted either nothing or very little of this pleasure.[1]

And because a power is naturally inclined to its good and to that which gives it pleasure, it happens that certain men of contemplation who are well fitted for the sciences from the side of their body and soul and are not prevented from [pursuing] these by external concerns begin to inquire in depth about that which they are pondering and wonder about the absence of a cause. Thus certain ones have recently wondered considerably how in a dream a man can have foreknowledge of future events about which he has never thought. They were urgently pressing me to tell them in writing what can be known through a dream and how it can be known.[2]

In giving in to their entreaties I shall first inquire whether science through dreams is possible, or whether through his dreams a man can have knowledge of future events.

On the one hand, it seems that such is not possible.

1.   Science as it exists in us is an effect of certain or of probable argumentation. But there is neither certain nor probable argumentation that someone who dreams about the rising of the moon in the heaven should have his own fame increased, or that someone who dreams about the setting of the sun should suffer a decrease in fame, as the ancient philosophers [and] diviners of dreams have held.[3]

2.   Moreover, of all the dreams which appear to us when we are asleep, some are present in us through phantasms received when we

---

[1] See above (p. 29) for Boethius's remarks in his *On the Supreme Good* concerning the supreme good available to man through use of his speculative intellect and through his practical intellect. Also, for the points that "sorrow when joined to an action shortens" it and "delight when joined to an action prolongs" it see his *Quaestiones super librum Topicorum*, Corpus Philosophorum Danicorum Medii Aevi, 6.1 (Copenhagen, 1976), 2, c. 6, qu. 25, p. 153: 14-18.

[2] This remark suggests that Boethius wrote this treatise in response to personal inquiries. Hence it probably should not be regarded as part of a longer set of questions on Aristotle's *De sommo et vigilia* (which at that time included three short Aristotelian treatises — *De sommo et vigilia, De insomniis, De divinatione per somnum*) which would have resulted from Boethius's public lectures as a Master in the Arts Faculty. See G. Fioravanti, "La 'scientia sompnialis' di Boezio di Dacia," pp. 334-335; Green-Pedersen, Introduction to his edition of this treatise, pp. lxi-lxii. This is not to say that Boethius did not perhaps deliver and publish such a set of questions as well; but if he did so, it has yet to be discovered.

[3] Cf. Albert the Great, *De sommo et vigilia* 3, tr. 1, c. 2 (Borgnet ed., 9: 179).

are awake and preserved in our soul; but others are produced in us through images which the imagination forms in us when we are asleep and subject to passions of the soul or body.[4] But we cannot know future events through dreams which are produced in the first way, since a phantasm does not give knowledge of anything except under the aspect of the present; nor through dreams produced in us in the second way, since the imagination does not know anything under the aspect of the future. Therefore, an image which the imagination forms in us when we are asleep does not pertain to anything under the aspect of the future. Therefore such an appearance in a dream cannot lead us to a knowledge of future events.

3.   Moreover, whatever we know we know either by learning it [through being taught] or by discovering it. But one who is asleep does not acquire knowledge of future events by discovery for he is not then giving himself to speculation about things; nor by learning, since he is not then giving himself to learning [through being taught] as is evident. Therefore, etc.

On the other hand, the opposite seems to be the case:

1.   because there is hardly a man who has not had a dream which tells something about the future, as everyone experiences within himself. For one who dreams and then arises often finds things to be in fact just as he has dreamed.[5]

[SOLUTION]

It must be said that knowledge through dreams or divination about the future through dreams is possible. In order for us to understand perfectly through which dreams future events cannot be known and for what reason, and through which dreams future events can be

---

[4] Here the term "phantasms" is used to translate the Latin *phantasmata*, and "images" to translate *idola*. By the first Boethius seems to have in mind the kind of sense-image which is produced (presumably by an inner sense) as a result of our direct perception of something. By the second he seems rather to have in mind something formed by the imagination which does not entail direct perception of a corresponding object by the external senses.

[5] See Aristotle, *De divinatione per somnum*, c. 1 (462b 14-15); Averroes, *Compendium libri Aristotelis De sompno et vigilia*, ed. A. L. Shields (Cambridge, Mass., 1949), p. 94:26-29 (*versio vulg.*); p. 94:25-29 (*versio Parisina*).

known and in what way, it must be noted that of the dreams which appear to us when we are asleep, some are coincidences. These have no connection with a future event, but are related to a future event in the way that lightning occurs while someone is walking.[6] Just as lightning sometimes occurs while someone is walking even though there is no connection between the two, so too, something sometimes appears in a dream to someone who later sees a similar event in reality outside the soul even though there is no connection between the one and the other. The event would have happened even if there had been no appearance similar to it in a dream, just as when lightning takes place while someone is walking, the lightning would still have happened even if he were not walking. And just as by walking one does not arrive at knowledge that lightning is to occur, so too through such dreams nothing can be divined about the future; with respect to it such dreams are coincidences.

And if you ask how such dreams are caused, I reply that [they are caused] through phantasms which are received by us when we are awake and which are preserved in the soul. While we are sleeping and while external motions have come to a halt and even the motion of rising vapors has lost its force, when such phantasms appear to the imagination, their appearance is a dream. And through such dreams one is especially likely to be deceived; for when one who has such a dream awakes, he sometimes sees a thing a phantasm of which he has seen in sleep, and believes that he now sees that thing because its phantasm appeared to him in sleep. In fact this is not so, as is clear, nor does the converse obtain. And if he should have recalled his dream before he saw that thing, he would believe that because of the dream he ought to see that thing, though it is evident that this is not the case. Therefore it happens that many things appear to those who are asleep, the like of which are never realized outside the mind in reality. This happens only in the way described.

These dreams as they happen more frequently are concerned with things which cannot be done by us. Something similar happens when we are awake. If someone is walking along a road and thinks of rain or of an eclipse and suddenly while he is thinking the thing which he was considering comes to pass, it is clear that the thing does not

---

[6] See Aristotle, *De divinatione per somnum*, c. 1 (462b 32).

occur because he is thinking of it, nor vice versa. So too, when someone who is sleeping sees the phantasm of an eclipse or of a rainbow and upon awakening immediately sees an eclipse or rainbow, it is clear that it is not because these things appeared to him in a dream that he now sees them; nor is it because he now sees them that he dreamed of them. [Rather he dreamed] of them because of phantasms of them which had previously been received and preserved in his soul and which appeared to him while he was sleeping and while internal and external motions had come to a halt, as has been said. For greater motions frequently prevent the perception of lesser ones. Through dreams of this kind, therefore, one does not divine about the future; but through these deception occurs, and the reason for this has been stated. These are produced in us in the way indicated. From what has been said it is also clear why many of those things which appear to those who are asleep never come to pass in external reality.[7]

There are other dreams, however, which are a cause of future events. As when a man who is thinking deeply about some action while he is asleep then remembers that action, so too, a phantasm of something which he can do sometimes appears to a man when he is asleep, and he works out that thing and a way of doing it within himself in his sleep. Upon awakening he remembers his dream and judges that the action is good along with its *modus agendi* [and] then performs it just as it was preconceived in his dream. Such a dream is a cause of future events, because if the phantasms of such things which he can perform had not appeared to him in his sleep, he would not have proceeded to carry them out. Therefore through such a dream one may know future events; for causes make known their effects.[8]

Among dreams, others are signs of future events. And certain of these dreams are caused in us by an external cause, as on some occasions by some constellation which alters the [transparent] medium up to the point of the body of the one who is asleep. As a result, if a great or a small amount of heat is produced in the body of the one who sleeps — because small motions seem to be great to those who are asleep since the soul is not concerned with other motions which

---

[7] Cf. ibid., c. 1 (463b 9-10).
[8] Ibid., c. 1 (463a 21-30).

impede these — when the imaginative power perceives this it forms an image which is appropriate for that passion, and the sleeper dreams that he is walking through fire.[9]

And if a strong cooling effect is produced in the body of the sleeper in the aforementioned manner, when the imaginative power perceives this and together with this on some occasions perceives a motion produced by a phantasm which was previously received there and preserved in the soul, the imagination forms an image of these things which are conjoined in a more suitable way than is possible [in reality].[10] For this is of the nature of the imagination, to form an image in the imitation and likeness of a thing whose motion it perceives. For this reason it is called the imaginative power. And then one who is asleep dreams that he is walking through snows, etc.

But after being awakened, as far as his dream is concerned and unless ignorance on the part of the sleeper prevents this, he can be aware of the present passion of his body upon which the form of his dream followed. From an effect it is possible to infer something about its cause. And through the passion which he knew through his dream he can also recognize the constellation, or something else, by which that passion was caused, and for the same reason. And because that passion of the body upon which the form of his dream followed can cause some future effect in his body, such as health or sickness, therefore through that passion the dreamer can know future effects, which [passion] he knew through his dream. Therefore, through a dream one can know future things, that is, those which such a passion causes.

But such a passion can be impeded from its action, and therefore its effect, of which the dream could be a sign, can fail to take place. In things which are done by choice, many of those things which are properly disposed to occur are changed when a weightier counsel intervenes. So too it frequently happens in things which are done by nature that many of those which are properly disposed to occur so far as their natural causes are concerned are prevented from taking place when a stronger and contrary cause intervenes which corrupts

[9] See ibid, c. 1 (463a 10-11); c. 2 (464a 16-18).
[10] On "phantasm" and "image" see note 4 above.

them. Therefore when the natural philosopher draws a conclusion in syllogistic fashion by means of such causes, that is, causes which can be impeded, he establishes his conclusion insofar as it follows from those causes, but does not establish it without qualification; for the causes through which he draws his conclusion can be impeded.

Thus a physician may reason: "He in whose body there is raw and undigested superfluous humor will die. Socrates is of this kind." The physician correctly demonstrates his conclusion insofar as it follows from this cause, but he does not demonstrate it without qualification. A warm medicine or a constellation or some other cause which strengthens the digestive heat will corrupt the cause from which the physician was arguing and thereby falsify his conclusion.

And this is why many are deceived in thinking that natural philosophers wish to demonstrate some conclusions in the unqualified sense when they demonstrate them by means of causes with respect to which or under the supposition of which it is not possible for those conclusions not to follow. But since those causes and consequently those conclusions can be otherwise — for the causes can be impeded — therefore natural philosophers do not intend to demonstrate such conclusions in the unqualified sense.[11]

In mathematics, however, one cause does not impede another, because mathematicals insofar as they are mathematicals are separate from motion. That a line which intersects with another line in perpendicular fashion forms two right angles, or that lines which are equally distant [from one another] do not intersect, such a cause can be impeded by no other cause. Therefore mathematical demonstrations enjoy the highest degree of certainty, and natural demonstrations come after these, as is evident from the above.

Among dreams others are caused in us from our side. Some of these are caused from the side of the body as when someone, who is overheated either from nourishment he has taken or from the matter of some fever, dreams that he is in fire. Small motions produced within the soul appear to sleepers to be great for the reason already mentioned.[12] And when vapors which are choleric, reddish, and burnt

---

[11] The reader will recall how central this point is to Boethius's discussion of the natural philosopher in his treatise *On the Eternity of the World*. See above, p. 52.

[12] For this point in Aristotle see note 9 above.

ascend to the organ of the imaginative power, a sleeper dreams that he is seeing flames and great fires. And when black and earthly vapors rise up, then the sleeper dreams that he is seeing black monks [i.e., Benedictines]; and certain foolish ones, having awakened, swear that they have seen devils while they were asleep. Sometimes, when clear vapors rise up to the organ of the imagination and are fashioned in different ways in their motions, at the same moment both the phantasms of white light and of sounds which were previously received and preserved in the soul move the power of the imagination. Then those who are sleeping dream that they are seeing brilliant places and angels singing and dancing. And when they have awakened they swear that they were carried away[13] and have in truth seen angels. And they are deceived because they are ignorant of the causes of things. And in the same way it happens to those who are sick, as to human beings suffering from grave illnesses so that their rational judgment is impaired, that once their suffering is lessened, they say to those around them that angels or devils have been present, and that they have seen many wonderful things.

And all of this is in accord with the different things which appear to the ill in the organ of the imagination when they are subject to such passions, that is, either to sleep or to illnesses. And although such cases of deception can happen owing to natural causes, nonetheless I do not deny that by divine will an angel or a devil can in truth appear to a person who is sleeping or to one who is ill.[14]

Some also wonder why the same thing seems to sleepers to change into different figures, as when it seems to a sleeper that he is seeing a black devil and suddenly the thing which appears to him is changed into a man and into many other things, as it seems to him. I say that the reason for this is that the earthly and black vapor or fume which rises and moves the imagination takes on different shapes in its motion. And it seems to the sleeper that it is changed into different

---

[13] "...iurant se raptos fuisse." This may have the technical meaning: they swear that they were in rapture, i.e., enjoying a certain level of prophetic knowledge. On this see Thomas Aquinas, *Summa theologiae* II-IIae, q. 171, Introd., and q. 175, a. 1.

[14] See the Condemnation of 1277, prop. 33 (*Chartularium*)/177 (Mandonnet): "That raptures and visions do not take place except through nature." See our Introduction above, p. 23, and notes 40, 41.

things because one who is asleep judges the phantasm of a thing to be the very thing itself. In like fashion, when someone sees that a cloud has the shape of a man or a lion, it is suddenly changed into another figure in its motion owing to the compression of a white and watery cloud with a black and earthly cloud.[15] And sometimes when it seems to a sleeper that he sees something black, it is suddenly changed and appears to him to be red. And I say this is so sometimes because the phantasms of things which have been previously received and preserved in the soul move the imagination of one who is asleep in succeeding fashion. And sometimes this is also because a black earthly vapor first arises and moves the imagination of the sleeper, and after it so does a burnt and choleric vapor in accord with the diversity of the matter which is turning into vapor and of the heat which is rising.

And because through dreams it is thus possible to know present passions to which dreamers are subject and future effects which can be caused from those passions, therefore dreams of the sick should be made known to skilled physicians. Through them one can know present passions to which the ill are subject and future effects which will follow from these passions, unless they are impeded.[16] For the passion of a dreamer conveys the form of the dream according to which form the appearance — which is the dream — is produced. The imagination forms a phantasm which corresponds to such a passion, just as when someone speaks to you, your imaginative power forms images of the things about which he is speaking and which you understand from his words. Otherwise you could not understand those things, since intelligibles are not produced in us except from things which are imagined.

Certain dreams are produced in us from the side of the soul.[17] Thus when a sleeper is subject to a strong passion of fear or of love,

---

[15] For Aristotle cf. *De somniis*, c. 3 (461b 19-21).

[16] See Aristotle, *De divinatione per somnum*, c. 1 (463a 5-6). Cf. Thomas Aquinas, *Summa theologiae* II-IIae, qu. 95, a. 6, for this and for other points of similarity with Boethius's treatise.

[17] In the immediately preceding paragraphs Boethius has been dealing with dreams which are caused in us from our side (rather than by some external cause) from the side of the body. See pp. 74-76. Now he turns to others which are caused in us from the side of the soul.

his imaginative power forms images which correspond to these passions such as a phantasm of an enemy or of his beloved, and he dreams about them. Upon arising he can divine the passion to which he was subject and also the effect which that passion could cause. And also, when he is suffering from a strong passion of fear, if in sleep he sees a phantasm of a friend, he is deceived so as to believe he is seeing his enemy because of the passion to which he is subject.[18] For the soul is moved by its own motion,[19] and that motion impedes the motion of the phantasm. Thus when someone who is awake is subject to a strong passion of fear, at every motion he believes his enemy is present. And when he sees someone from afar, he believes that he is seeing his enemy even though what he sees bears little resemblance to his enemy. So too, when a man thinks strongly about some thing, he believes that all whom he hears speaking are speaking about that thing.

Some are accustomed to be in doubt concerning why dreams do not happen in children, or why monstrous dreams [do].[20] I say the reason for this is that children are subject to considerable heat and their food itself has much vapor; for they do not use coarse nourishment which turns into vapor only with difficulty. Therefore much upward motion of vapor prevents images from appearing and thus a dream does not take place. And if it does occur, it makes confused things appear and then a monstrous dream is produced, and children are immediately awakened in tears because they are frightened by their dreams. Something similar happens in water in which, if it is strongly stirred, the countenance of the one watching it does not appear at all. If it is gently moved, the countenance appears, but in confused fashion. If, however, the water is at rest, then the countenance of the viewer appears as it is.[21] It is also for this reason that dreams do

---

[18] Cf. Aristotle, *De somniis*, c. 2 (460b 4-8).

[19] I.e., the passion of fear.

[20] This final paragraph may be regarded as a particular problem (*dubium*) which Boethius has appended to the "Solution" (*corpus*) of his treatise. Interestingly, Boethius does not seem to have judged it necessary to reply to the three opening arguments he had presented (see pp. 69-70 above). Perhaps he felt that he had already done so sufficiently in writing the *corpus*.

[21] Cf. Aristotle, *De somniis*, c. 3 (461a 11ff); *De divinatione per somnum*, c. 2 (464b 8-11).

not occur in men who sleep immediately after taking food, or if they do, the dreams are monstrous, because then there is much upward movement of vapor.[22] During the day when digestion is now, as it were, completed, proper dreams occur, since then the motion of nourishment ceases.

---

[22] See Aristotle, *De somniis*, c. 3 (461a 12ff., 462b 4ff.).

Bibliography

Works by Boethius of Dacia:

Boethii Daci Opera. Modi Significandi sive Quaestiones super Priscianum Maiorem. Ed. J. Pinborg, H. Roos, with S. Skovgaard Jensen. Corpus Philosophorum Danicorum Medii Aevi, 4.1. Copenhagen, 1969.

——. *Opuscula De aeternitate mundi, De summo bono, De somniis.* Ed. N. G. Green-Pedersen. Corpus Philosophorum Danicorum Medii Aevi, 6.2. Copenhagen, 1976.

——. *Quaestiones de Generatione.* Ed. Géza Sajó. Corpus Philosophorum Danicorum Medii Aevi, 5.1. Copenhagen, 1972.

——. *Quaestiones super libros Physicorum.* Ed. Géza Sajó. Corpus Philosophorum Danicorum Medii Aevi, 5.2. Copenhagen, 1974.

——. *Quaestiones super librum Topicorum.* Ed. N. G. Green-Pedersen and J. Pinborg. Corpus Philosophorum Danicorum Medii Aevi, 6.1. Copenhagen, 1976.

Boetii de Dacia Tractatus De aeternitate mundi. Ed. Géza Sajó. Berlin, 1964.

"Die Opuscula *De summo bono sive de vita philosophi* und *De sompniis* des Boetius von Dacien." Ed. Martin Grabmann. *Archives d'Histoire Doctrinale et Littéraire du Moyen Âge* 6 (1932), 287-317. Also in *Mittelalterliches Geistesleben* 2 (1936), 200-224. English tr. of this edition by John F. Wippel in John F. Wippel and Allan B. Wolter. *Medieval Philosophy: From St. Augustine to Nicholas of Cusa.* New York, 1969. Pp. 369-375.

Un traité récemment découvert de Boèce de Dacie De mundi aeternitate. Ed. Géza Sajó. Budapest, 1954.

Works by Other Authors:

Albert the Great. *De somno et vigilia.* In *Opera omnia.* Ed. A. Borgnet. Paris, 1890-99. Vol. 9.

Aristotle. *The Works of Aristotle.* Ed. W. D. Ross. Oxford University Press, 1908-1952.

Augustine. *De civitate dei.* Ed. B. Dombart and A. Kalb. Corpus Christianorum, Series Latina, Vols. 47, 48. Turnholt, 1955.

Averroes. *In Aristotelis opera cum Averrois commentariis.* Venice, 1562-1574; repr. Frankfurt, 1962.

—— *Compendium libri Aristotelis de sompno et vigilia*, in *Averrois Cordubensis Compendia librorum Aristotelis qui parva naturalia vocantur*. Ed. A. Ledyard Shields, with H. Blumberg. Cambridge, Mass., 1949.

Bataillon, Louis-Jacques. "Bulletin d'histoire des doctrines médiévaux: le treizième siècle (fin)." *Revue des Sciences Philosophiques et Théologiques* 65 (1981), 101-122.

Behler, Ernst. *Die Ewigkeit der Welt. Problemgeschichtliche Untersuchungen zu den Kontroversen um Weltanfang und Weltunendlichkeit in der arabischen und jüdischen Philosophie des Mittelalters*. Munich-Paderborn-Vienna, 1965.

Bianchi, Luca. *L'errore di Aristotele. La polemica contro l'eternità del mondo nel XIII secolo*. Florence, 1984.

Boethius. *The Theological Tractates. The Consolation of Philosophy*. Trs. H. F. Stewart, E. K. Rand, S. J. Tester. Cambridge, Mass., 1978.

Bonaventure. *Doctoris Seraphici S. Bonaventurae... Opera Omnia*. Quaracchi, 1882-1902.

"Condemnation of 219 Propositions." Tr. Ernst L. Fortin and Peter D. O'Neill. In *Medieval Political Philosophy: A Sourcebook*, ed. Ralph Lerner and Muhsin Mahdi, pp. 335-354. New York, 1963.

"The Condemnation of 1277." Tr. John Wellmuth. In *Philosophy in the West: Readings in Ancient and Medieval Philosophy*, ed. Joseph Katz and Rudolph H. Weingartner, pp. 532-542. New York, 1965.

Denifle, H. "Quellen zur Gelehrtengeschichte des Predigerordens im 13. und 14. Jahrhundert." *Archiv für Literatur- und Kirchengeschichte des Mittelalters* 2 (1886), 165-248.

Denifle, H. and Chatelain, A. *Chartularium Universitatis Parisiensis*. Paris, 1889. Vol. 1.

Dondaine, Antoine. "Le manuel de l'inquisiteur 1230-1330." *Archivum Fratrum Praedicatorum* 17 (1947), 85-194.

Fioravanti, Gianfranco. "La 'scientia sompnialis' di Boezio di Dacia." *Atti della Accademia delle Scienze di Torino. Classe di Scienze morale* 101 (1966-1967), 329-369.

Gauthier, René Antoine. "Notes sur Siger de Brabant: II. Siger en 1272-1275, Aubry de Reims et la scission des Normands." *Revue des Sciences Philosophiques et Théologiques* 68 (1984), 1-49.

Gilson, Etienne. "Boèce de Dacie et la double vérité." *Archives d'Histoire Doctrinale et Littéraire du Moyen Âge* 20 (1955), 81-99.

——. *History of Christian Philosophy in the Middle Ages*. New York, 1955.

Godfrey of Fontaines. *Les Quodlibet Cinq, Six et Sept de Godefroid de Fontaines*. Ed. Maurice De Wulf and Jean Hoffmans. Les Philosophes Belges, 3. Louvain, 1914.

——. *Le huitième Quodlibet, Le neuvième Quodlibet, Le dixième Quodlibet.* Ed. Jean Hoffmans. Les Philosophes Belges, 4. Louvain, 1924, 1928, 1931.

Godfrey of Fontaines' Abridgement of Boethius of Dacia's Modi Significandi sive Quaestiones Super Priscianum Maiorem. Tr. A. Charlene Senape McDermott. Amsterdam Studies in the Theory and History of Linguistic Science, 3: Studies in the History of Linguistics, Vol. 22. Amsterdam, 1980.

Grabmann, Martin. *Neuaufgefundene Werke des Siger von Brabant und Boetius von Dacien.* Sitzungsberichte der Bayerischen Akademie der Wissenschaften. Philosophisch-historische Abteilung, 1924, 2. Munich, 1924.

Hauréau, B. "Un des hérétiques condamnés à Paris en 1277." *Journal des Savants* (1886), 176-183.

——. "Boetius, maître ès arts à Paris." *Histoire littéraire de la France* 30 (1888), 270-279.

Hissette, Roland. "Albert le Grand et Thomas d'Aquin dans la censure parisienne du 7 mars 1277." *Miscellanea Mediaevalia* 15 (Berlin, 1982), 226-246.

——. *Enquête sur les 219 articles condamnés à Paris le 7 mars 1277.* Louvain-Paris, 1977.

——. "Etienne Tempier et ses condamnations." *Recherches de Théologie ancienne et médiévale* 47 (1980), 231-270.

Jensen, S. Skovgaard. "On the National Origin of the Philosopher Boetius de Dacia." *Classica et Mediaevalia* 24 (1963), 232-241.

Laporta, Jorge. *La destinée de la nature humaine selon Thomas d'Aquin.* Paris, 1965.

Le Liber de Causis. Édition établie à l'aide de 90 manuscrits avec Introduction et Notes. Ed. Adriaan Pattin. Leuven, n.d. Also in *Tijdschrift voor Filosofie* 28 (1966), 90-203.

Litt, Thomas. *Les corps célestes dans l'univers de saint Thomas d'Aquin.* Louvain-Paris, 1963.

Mandonnet, Pierre. "Note complémentaire sur Boèce de Dacie." *Revue des Sciences Philosophiques et Théologiques* 22 (1933), 246-250.

——. *Siger de Brabant et l'averroïsme latin au XIIIᵉ siècle.* 2d ed., 2 Vols. Louvain, 1911, 1908.

Maurer, Armand. "Boethius of Dacia and the Double Truth." *Mediaeval Studies* 17 (1955), 235-239.

——. "Siger of Brabant on Fables and Falsehoods in Religion." *Mediaeval Studies* 43 (1981), 515-530.

Meersseman, G. *Laurentii Pignon Catalogi et Chronica, accedunt Catalogi Stamsensis et Upsalensis scriptorum O.P.* Rome, 1936.

Moses Maimonides. *The Guide of the Perplexed.* Tr. and intr. by Shlomo Pines; introd. essay by Leo Strauss. Chicago, 1963.

Owens, Joseph. *Human Destiny. Some Problems for Catholic Philosophy.* Washington, D.C., 1985.

"The Parisian Condemnations of 1270." In *Medieval Philosophy: From St. Augustine to Nicholas of Cusa*, ed. John F. Wippel and Allan B. Wolter, p. 366. New York, 1969.

Pinborg, Jan. "Zur Philosophie des Boethius de Dacia. Ein Uberblick." *Studia Mediewistyczne* 15 (1974), 165-185.

St. Thomas Aquinas, Siger of Brabant, St. Bonaventure: On the Eternity of the World. Tr. Cyril Vollert, Lottie H. Kendzierski, Paul M. Byrne. Milwaukee, 1964.

Sajó, Géza. "Boetius de Dacia und seine philosophische Bedeutung." *Miscellanea Mediaevalia* 2 (Berlin, 1963), 454-463.

Sassen, F. "Boethius van Dacie en de Theorie van de dubbele waarheid." *Studia Catholica* 30 (1955), 266-273.

Schrödter, Hermann. "Boetius von Dacien und die Autonomie des Wissens. Ein Fund und seine Bedeutung." *Theologie und Philosophie* 47 (1972), 16-35.

Siger of Brabant. *Quaestiones in Tertium de Anima, De anima intellectiva, De aeternitate mundi.* Ed. B. Bazán. Louvain-Paris, 1972.

Thomas Aquinas. *Opera omnia.* Leonine ed., Rome, 1882 —.

——. *The Division and Methods of the Sciences. Questions V and VI of his Commentary on the 'De Trinitate' of Boethius.* Tr. Armand Maurer. 3d rev. ed. Toronto, 1963.

——. *Expositio super librum Boethii De Trinitate.* Ed. Bruno Decker. Ed. altera, Leiden, 1959.

——. *Quaestiones disputatae de potentia.* Ed. P. M. Pession. Turin-Rome, 1953.

——. *Quaestiones Quodlibetales.* Ed. R. Spiazzi. Turin-Rome, 1956.

——. *Scriptum super libros Sententiarum.* Ed. P. Mandonnet and M. F. Moos. 4 vols. Paris, 1929-1947.

Van Steenberghen, Fernand. "Une légende tenace: la théorie de la double vérité." *Académie Royale de Belgique. Bulletin de la Classe des Lettres.* Sér. 5, 56 (1970), 179-196. Repr. in his *Introduction à l'étude de la philosophie médiévale.* Louvain-Paris, 1974. Pp. 555-570.

——. *Maître Siger de Brabant.* Louvain-Paris, 1977.

——. "Nouvelles recherches sur Siger de Brabant et son école." *Revue philosophique de Louvain* 54 (1956), 130-147.

——. *La philosophie au XIIIe siècle.* Louvain, 1966.

——. *Thomas Aquinas and Radical Aristotelianism.* Washington, D.C., 1980.

Weisheipl, James A. "The Date and Context of Aquinas' *De aeternitate mundi.*" In *Graceful Reason: Essays in Ancient and Medieval Philosophy Presented to Joseph Owens, CSSR*, ed. Lloyd P. Gerson, pp. 239-271. Toronto, 1983.

——. *Friar Thomas d'Aquino. His Life, Thought and Works*, With *Corrigenda* and *Addenda*. Washington, D.C., 1983.

——. "The Nature, Scope, and Classification of the Sciences." In *Science in the Middle Ages*, ed. David C. Lindberg, pp. 461-482. Chicago, 1978.

Wieland, Georg. *Ethica — Scientia Practica. Die Anfänge der philosophischen Ethik im 13. Jahrhundert.* Beiträge zur Geschichte der Philosophie und Theologie des Mittelalters, Neue Folge, 21. Münster, 1981.

Wilpert, Paul. "Boethius von Dacien — die Autonomie des Philosophen." *Miscellanea Mediaevalia* 3 (Berlin, 1964), 135-152.

Wippel, John F. "The Condemnations of 1270 and 1277 at Paris." *The Journal of Medieval and Renaissance Studies* 7 (1977), 169-201.

——. "Did Thomas Aquinas Defend the Possibility of an Eternally Created World? (The *De aeternitate mundi* Revisited)." *Journal of the History of Philosophy* 19 (1981), 21-37. Repr. as Ch. 8 of following item.

——. *Metaphysical Themes in Thomas Aquinas.* Washington, D.C., 1984.

——. *The Metaphysical Thought of Godfrey of Fontaines: A Study in Late Thirteenth-Century Philosophy.* Washington, D.C., 1981.

Index of Names

Index of Subjects

Printed by the workers
of Editions Marquis, Montmagny Québec,
in February 1987